ARJUN:

The life - story of an Indian boy

ARJUN:

The life - story of an Indian boy

S. E. STOKES

GYAN

Published by

Gyan Publishing House
5, Ansari Road
Daryaganj, New Delhi-110002
Phone: 011-47034999, 9811692060
E-mail: books@gyanbooks.com

Distribution Network
gyanbooks.com
India, USA, Canada, UK, Australia

ISBN: 978-93-6433-172-2 (HB)

First Published, 1910

2nd Impression 2024

Printed at: Gyan Press, Delhi.

ARJUN:
The life - story of an Indian boy
Author: S. E. STOKES

ARJUN

The life-story of an Indian boy

THREE MEN FROM ARJUN'S VILLAGE.

ARJUN

The life-story of an Indian boy

BY

S. E. STOKES

OF THE BROTHERHOOD OF THE IMITATION OF JESUS

ILLUSTRATED

Society for the Propagation of the Gospel in Foreign Parts

WESTMINSTER

1910

PREFACE

THIS book, which was written primarily for young people, will be found full of interest by those who are grown up. Some of the information relating to the curious customs of the mountain people to the north-west of Simla has never before been printed. The writer, who is an American, went out to India some years ago, and after spending a year in nursing lepers and dressing their wounds, gave away all that he possessed, and wandered from place to place, trusting entirely to the hospitality of the people, nursing those who were dying of the plague, and trying to interpret to them the meaning of the love of Jesus. He has now been joined by several others, Indians and Europeans, and has founded the Brotherhood of the Imitation of Jesus. His work is chiefly amongst those who belong to the highest castes in India, to whom missionary work carried on on ordinary lines appeals least. The story is a true one, and the boy whose life is described (though his name is altered) is now studying at an Indian University. We ask the earnest prayers of all who read this story for the members of this Brotherhood and their work.

C. H. ROBINSON.

S.P.G. HOUSE,
January, 1910.

CONTENTS

b

LIST OF ILLUSTRATIONS

ARJUN.

THE LIFE STORY OF AN INDIAN BOY.

I.

ARJUN'S HOME.

FAR back in the mountains behind Simla is a village called Zahu. It lies in a hollow on a mountain side, nestling in the midst of its tiny fields. Above are the houses of the Hindoos, Brahmins, Pujaris, Rajputs and Kanaits. There are fine houses, two or three stories high, built of stone, and strengthened with great beams of wood laid in the stonework. They have lovely little porches too, built close up under the eaves, far out of reach of snow and the defiling hands of strangers. On the upper floor the people dwell, and on the ground floor they keep their cows and goats. If the house has three stories, the middle is used for a storeroom to hold the winter's grain, the unspun wool and the farm implements.

A little below the houses of the Hindoos is

(2000/O.8957)

another group of dwellings. These are much humbler in appearance, and not so clean or tidy. They are the homes of the lower castes, the workers in iron and leather, and the coolies, who are the serfs of the landowners.

Below this group lie two or three wretched hovels, looking more like pig-pens than houses. In these dwell the Rhers, the people of the basket-weaving caste, who are looked upon as most unclean, and who act as the scavengers of the place.

There is one other building which it would be well to examine. It stands in a stone courtyard of its own, a little to the right of the group of houses which belong to the high-caste population of the village. The first thing which strikes us is its great height; it looks almost like a tower as it stands overlooking the place. It has a porch up under the roof like the other houses, but the wood of the porch and the ends of the roof beams are elaborately carved. Any one acquainted with the mountain villagers who live between Simla and Tibet would be able to tell you at once that this is the "Deora," the house of the local god.

Such a place is the village of Zahu, hanging on its hillside in the midst of its terraced fields, and looking out over the purple valleys of the Himalayas to the Tibetan mountains, a hundred miles

THE VILLAGE OF DEORA WHERE THE GOD IS KEPT. THE LITTLE PORCH CAN BE SEEN UNDER THE ROOF.

away. Above it and to one side of it lies a forest of oak and pines and cedar, stretching up to the ridge. And far below it one can see other villages and other fields. And below them far down in the valley lies the river Sutlej, looking like a narrow ribbon of silver as it flows where the rice-fields are gloriously green and the fever is most deadly.

Nihal Singh, the Rajput, was one of the first men of Zahu. He was of the same caste and family as the Raja of his State, and had been granted peculiar privileges on that account. Moreover, he was the possessor of many broad fields and a fine house; and for many generations his forefathers had been the custodians of an image of Parmeshari, the goddess mother of Kali Mai, which was held in peculiar veneration throughout that part of the country. Parmeshari dwelt in her own room, next to the living-room of the family, and Nihal Singh was not the only one who believed that she guarded the house of her adoption safe from the malice of man and demons.

The Rajput had two children, a boy and a girl. It is with the life of this boy that our story has to deal.

Great was the rejoicing at his birth. Nihal

Singh looked upon the event as a manifest sign of the good-will of Maha Deo and of Sankra Bir, whose image stood in the threshing-floor behind the house. They called the baby Arjun Singh, after his ancestor, the heroic prince Arjun, and his mother, at least, thought that the leader of the Pandua was highly honoured in having such an absolutely perfect baby named after him.

What shall we say of the first months of Arjun's life? It was very much like that of all other babies, wherever their homes may be. He grew bigger and fatter and hungrier and jollier every day; and before many months had passed he learned to crawl, in his earnest desire to catch a certain sunbeam which was in the habit of creeping slowly across the floor of the room and up the wall each day.

When he was about a year old, all the people of the village came together to rejoice with the father over the birth of his son. Nihal Singh had prepared the Badáí for them, pieces of cloth and food for the Brahmins and other high castes, and money for the humbler people. There was dancing, and song, and laughter, and a great beating of drums that day, and at the end of it the people went happily home with their gifts.

As the years went by Arjun grew into a sturdy, bright-faced child. Like all small boys, he divided his time between playing, and eating, and sleeping. Sometimes he would sit silently by his mother, watching her solemnly, as with deft hands she shaped the flat round native bread and put it on the tawo to bake. Then he would go out behind the house, and squatting down beside a chula (oven) of his own making, would make little flat round cakes of mud and cook them over an imaginary fire. Every day his father was in the habit of doing puja (worship) before the image of Parmeshari. This always interested Arjun very much, and he asked many questions about it. Why did his father stand there night and morning talking that way? Did Parmeshari hear? When he became a man could he also do puja? And many more questions of a like nature he asked.

Year by year Arjun's father kept the Shio ratri, the great festival of the god Shio. On the evening of the twentieth day he prepared the mandal, in the great living-room of the family. First he made a figure with wheat-flour on the floor. It looked like the hub and spokes of a carriage-wheel. On the end of each spoke he sprinkled the flour so as to look like a flower.

Then he drew two circles, one inside the figure around the hub, and one outside the figure and surrounding it. Then on the hub he heaped up a great pile of grain, and on top of this he placed a little earthen cup, filled with oil, with a wick burning in it. After this he made the rough figure of a goat out of rice, and placed it with its mouth in the oil. At each point where one of the spokes crossed the inner circle he placed a little heap of grain, a different kind of grain on every spoke, and on one of these piles he placed a little mud image of the god Shio. Then he filled all the space between the two circles with finely cooked food, in one place putting two large loaves of Indian bread, and near them the head of a goat.

All this Nihal Singh prepared, singing the while "The Song of Kiru," and Arjun, sitting quietly in a corner of the great room, looked on with wide eyes, wondering. Next day they missed the child, and after a brief search found him solemnly making a mandal of his own with dust and pebbles. And on a little heap of earth the childish hands had placed a mud figure of the god Shio.

When the boy was about six years old his mother and father took him up to a place on the

JACH, THE VILLAGE GOD OF ZAHU. THE MEN SITTING ROUND ARE THE POOR PEOPLE OF THE PLACE WHO CARRY IT.

top of the hill which overhung the village. The name of the place was Koti Sharai; it was open and a great tree stood at one side of it. Here were assembled a number of other boys of about the same age, with their parents. There were priests also, and Jach, the village god, had been brought to grace the occasion. Then there was a great reading of books and repeatings of mantras (mystic verses), and one of the priests cut the children's hair, leaving nothing but the bods, the long tuft of hair which every male Hindoo wears on the top of his head. Then there was a feast of rice and goat's meat, and bread dripping with ghi (clarified butter).

From this time Arjun may be said to have entered upon his boyhood. At first he played near the house, and helped his mother, or went with his father or one of his uncles on their various trips to the mill, or smithy, or shop. And two or three times a year Nihal Singh would dress him in his best clothes, and take him to one of the melas, or local fairs, where men and boys, forming in long lines, did the mountain-dance before the images of their gods, and ate sweets, and drank the liquor which hillmen make from gurli (sugar). The mela-days were the joy of Arjun's life—the walk through wood and field with laughing crowds of fellow-villagers, gaily dressed for the occasion and bent upon enjoying themselves; the solemn dance before the gods, when he proudly clutched his father's hand and imitated his every movement; the excitement of buying sweets, and mingling in with talk and laughter; the deep boom of the dhol (a large native drum), and the rasping blare of the great trumpets. Arjun sighed with regret that life was not a continual round of melas.

And so the months and years slipped by until the boy was ten years old. And a fine-looking lad he was, with the broad forehead and delicate features of the high-caste Hindoo. He was a boy, too, with a character of his own. At times he would seem to simply bubble over with fun and mischief, and he would then lead the boys of the village into all sorts of scrapes and boyish adventures. At such times he was their recognised leader, and they followed him with the devotion and whole-hearted admiration which only boys can give. But there were times—even in the midst of their wildest pranks—when their companion's face would lose its smile and his eyes would become thoughtful and sad; then they would steal away and leave him to himself, instinctively feeling that something had risen up

TWO OF THE MOUNTAIN GODS.

between him and them, and that they would have nothing in common until he had become his own happy self again. As for his parents, they simply adored their boy, and felt that he was destined to do great things.

II.

ARJUN GOES TO SCHOOL.

One day, when Arjun was about twelve years old, his father said to him, "Son, thou art now of an age to share the burden of the house, and I shall send thee out with Shama, Hiru's lad, to graze the goats".

Nihal Singh then went to the family priest and said, "Oh! Parohotji, make, a jantar (charm) for my son, which will keep at a distance every bhut, pret, or other evil spirit which might otherwise do him harm". So the priest made the jantar, and put it into a little bag—long strips of paper with mantras written on them, the rough picture of a lion, an astronomic chart, and some ashes. And Nihal Singh hung it about the neck of his son.

"This will protect thee from all demons save only the Banshira," he said. And he told the lad how to guard himself against the forest demon which hillmen fear the most. "And, remember, he will come to thee in form as one of thy friends;

A VIEW OVER THE SUTLEJ RIVER, FROM RAMPUR, NEAR KULU.

and he will call to thee from a distance so," and he gave the call. "Therefore give no answer to any one until thou hast seen his feet, or until he has called thee thrice. For the Banshira will differ in nothing from one of thy friends saving in this, that from the knees his feet will be set on backward, with calves to the front: this sign is sure. Nor does the Banshira ever call three times; therefore, if one call thee more than twice thou mayest safely answer. If thou answereth him, nothing can save thee." And Arjun promised, and never answered a friend until he had called three times or shown his feet.

Those were happy months which he spent with the goats. Sometimes he and Shama were alone all day, sometimes they grazed their goats in company with other boys. What games they had! Now they would be kings travelling in state through their dominions, another time they would be road builders, and would dig out little roads upon the hillside, with here a tunnel and there a paraon (the halting-place on an Indian road), with tiny shops of mud and grass about it. Or they would lie on their backs and tell each other the stories which they had heard from their elders of fairies and demons, gods and kings. Or they would sing lamarus—the weird, long-drawn-out, quavering songs of the mountains, which end with a sudden rising inflection—and listen to hear them taken up by some one far away on another hillside. And thus they would spend their days following the slowly grazing goats, until the long shadows creeping up the hillsides warned them that it was time to be getting home.

As the winter drew on Arjun and his companions ceased to be sent out with the goats. They fed them at home now with grass cut during the summer months. And they spent their time in other, yet not less enjoyable, ways. Nihal Singh taught his son how to spin into thread the grey wool purchased in the autumn at the great Rampur fair. To this day the boy remembers how they used to sit by the hour spinning in the firelight. And Nihal Singh would tell him story upon story of the ancient glory of the Rajputs—of Arjun and Bim, San and Ram Chandar, or tales of the mountain gods and demons. And the boy's eyes would grow big with wonder, and the darting shadows would appear to him as monsters trying to devour him as the fire flickered and burned low upon the hearth and the wind howled outside among the mountains.

TWO OF THE GODS AT ONE OF THE MOUNTAIN FAIRS,

"Yes," the father would say, puffing at his hooka (pipe) the while, "there be many kinds of demons—banshirs, mashan, jou, churèl, and gods not a few—who, when angered, are worse than a host of demons; but, god or devil, I know not one more dangerous to rouse than Sankra Bir."

"Sankra Bir who dwells in the old palace above us?" asked Arjun. "I have heard fearsome tales of him, and none of the boys dare approach the palace after sundown."

"The boys do well to fear the god," his father answered. "Once Sankra Bir was a devil, and to this day his nature is in part that of a devil. Guard the village he may, but woe betide the man who meets him at night, all white, and riding on a white horse! For this cause people fear to pass this house at night. For an image of the god has stood for hundreds of years at the back of our threshing-floor, and the priests say that he often frequents the place. In royal Sarahan, also, is a figure of Sankra, much reverenced and feared by the people of that place. They talk of a well also sacred to the god, and of how at the great mela the priests lead thither some simple-minded countrymen, and—but why should I scare thee with such dark tales, my son? Let me tell thee rather of the goddess

Bhima Kali." And he would launch out into a description of the goddess who appears only to the king and is invisible to every one else, and of the horse which is kept for her at Sarahan, that she may ride upon it before the sunrise. "Great is the goddess Bhima Kali," he would conclude, "and it is she who gives long life to the Rajas of Bushahr."

And thus with spinning of wool and telling of stories the winter passed away, and with the spring came warmer breezes, and thousands of mountain streamlets began to carry the melting snow down to the swollen Sutlej in the valley below. Then the men of the hills came out of their houses, like bees out of their hives, and girt themselves for the spring ploughing. The terraced fields around the villages became alive with workers. And on every side might be heard the voices of the ploughmen as they urged their tiny oxen to renewed efforts and drove their wooden ploughs through the soft, wet earth.

The spring brought a change for Arjun. His father was ambitious for him, and had no desire for him to remain simple and unlettered as the other village lads. There was a school at Khuni where twenty or more boys were busily learning, and it was decided that Arjun should go there

THE RAJA (KING) OF BUSHAHR.

also. So behold them—father and son—tramping along the path to the school early one Monday morning.

The school-house stands at the rear of the village, and just above the other houses. As Arjun drew near the door he could hear the boys studying their lessons. Indian boys all study their lessons aloud, and no one seems to be at all bothered by the noise. Indeed, if one visits a small village school in India, he will probably find two or three classes studying their lessons at the top of their voices, another class or two writing quietly on their whited wooden boards, and still another class reciting the day's lessons to the teacher. "What confusion!" foreigners would probably exclaim. Yes; but there is an order and method in it.

Arjun was given a seat on the floor with the beginners, a whited board, pen, ink, and a piece of cardboard with the letters of the Nagri alphabet printed upon it, and was ordered to copy them as neatly as possible on the whited board.

Poor boy! It was slow work at first, and for days it seemed as if his fingers were all thumbs. It was tiresome too. He much preferred the wind-blown hillsides and the games with the boys of his village, to making little black letters on a board, and having to rub them out again every day. Then it was much more fun to lie on one's back and sing songs in the open than to stand up before an exacting old school-teacher and sing the alphabet and the multiplication table.

At first he begged his father to take him away from school and set him to minding goats again. But Nihal Singh reminded him of the stock from which he was sprung, and told him to persevere. "Remember that thou art a Rajput of the got [a caste-division] of Sham, and that the blood of great kings runs in thy veins. Thy forefathers overcame mighty kings and powerful demons; great shame would it be if thou, their son, wert unable to conquer little black marks on a piece of wood. Sons of poor farmers and shopkeepers have gained this knowledge; wilt thou allow thyself to be overcome by such? Shame on thee, my son; persevere until thou hast acquired all that the Sala of Khuni can teach thee, and —who knows?—some day thou mayst be a Government servant, and draw as much as 20 rupees (24*s.*) a month."

And Arjun did persevere, and to such purpose that within a few months he became one of the best pupils in the school.

III.

HIS FIRST SORROW.

The first real sorrow which the lad had experienced came with the death of his mother. During the winter previous to his going to school she had taken a heavy cold which had settled on her lungs. For some weeks her friends had been very anxious about her, but she seemed to rally and they had hoped that her strength would come back to her with the warm weather. This was not the case, however; she lay listlessly on her bed, and grew weaker and weaker until it became manifest to all that they were about to lose her.

Nihal Singh and Arjun's aunt Gauri sat beside her, and the boy, his eyes wide with fear and distress, sat at her feet. It was a pitiful scene, for they had all truly loved the quiet, gentle little woman, who had so devotedly loved and served her husband and her little son and daughter. The latter was too young to understand, but Arjun was quite broken-hearted. He felt—poor little boy—that his mother was about to leave him, and that he would never again see her, or feel her warm love. There could be little comfort to him from the faith of his fathers, and no hope of a blessed reunion on the other side of death. He was losing her, and as she breathed her last, and they slipped the rupee between her lips to pay for entrance into the next world, he crept away into a corner, sobbing miserably.

Meanwhile the rumour that the Rajput's wife was dying had brought all the village together before the door of the house. Not one was missing, for to be absent from the marriage or funeral of any of one's fellow-villagers is a crime against the whole village community, and he who absents himself becomes very unpopular.

As soon as those outside heard that Arjun's mother was dead, they began to bestir themselves. A man started on the run for holy Karalius, the place of the great temple six miles away, to summon the Dhumnas with their great dhols (drums) and other instruments. Others went to the houses of the smith and the carpenter to tell them to bring their tools. A dozen or more repaired to the forest to cut the wood needful for the coffin and the funeral pyre.

THE WOMEN OF ZAHU.

Meanwhile those within the house were sewing up the body in fine cloth stuffs, preparing it for the burning, and as they worked they wailed.

And now the Dhumnas arrived with their drums—black-faced, wild-looking men, with long matted hair, thought by the hillmen to be half man, half jhou (vampire). Down they sat on the ground outside the house, and the deep, monotonous boom of their drums mingled with and rose above the voices of the mourners and the sharp sounds of the carpenters' hammers as they worked at the coffin.

The coffin which Haruja and Hiru, the carpenters, prepared upon this occasion was a very fine one, built of great deodar planks, and beautifully carved. It took almost all night to make it, and all the time the people lamented and the drums kept booming.

Early on the following morning groups of people could be seen approaching the village from various directions. They were the relatives and friends of the stricken family, and as they walked they wailed. Each group brought fine cloths, and laid them on the body.

When every one had arrived, and everything was ready, the body was taken out to be put in the box. As they brought it forth, with its head toward those without, and its feet toward the door, all the people set up a great wail, which could be heard far down the valley.

After they had laid it in the coffin, and placed on top of it the various articles of fine clothing which had been brought that day by the mourners, they filled the vacant corners with quantities of Indian sweets—ladu pehra and balu-shai.

Then the family priest drew near, and, making a little image of dough, placed it near the coffin. Next he poured water upon it, and repeated the proper shloks (Sanskrit verses) for the occasion.

This ceremony ended, the mourners took up the coffin, and the assembled crowd fell in behind it, and set off in long procession for the burning-place. Indar Singh, the fifteen-year-old son of Arjun's uncle, walked beside the coffin and waved a fan over the body.

When farmers bury their dead, its Dhumnas play a death march on their drums. But this was the funeral of a Rajput, and the advance of the body to the burning-place must be as the march of some great king or of a god. So the drums boomed out the Chatradand, and the sound of the royal advance went rolling down the valley.

They moved but slowly ; for, whenever there was a stream to be crossed, the family priest must needs make another little dough image, and, seating it upon a throne of flour, pour water upon it, and repeat more shloks.

When half the road had been covered the procession halted. The Dhumnas grouped themselves on one side of the coffin, and Nihal Singh and several other Rajputs, standing on the other side, cast handfuls of coppers across the body to them. A live ram was also thrown at them in the same way, and the procession resumed its march.

At length they drew near to the burning-place—a glade in the forest, with a stream of clear water running through it. Here a funeral pyre had been erected of dry wood. The coffin was placed on a flat rock, some more Sanskrit verses were repeated by the priest, and it was lifted on to the pyre.

Then old Haria the carpenter advanced with his axe and struck the box a blow. A splinter fell to the ground, and he picked it up and placed it behind his ear, that he might be able to look into the future and know who next would die.

Arjun's uncle touched the four corners of the pyre with a torch, the people returned sadly to the Rajput's house, and, after a word of comfort for the family, departed to their homes. Poor little

Arjun—his head shaved in token of mourning—crept home and sobbed himself to sleep in the desolate house.

Next day the potter came with pots, and the smith with a little iron ladder. And the priest performed the ceremony for sending the dead woman's soul to Heaven. And, that the soul should not be stopped at Betarni a cow was given to the priest, and sacred instructions were whispered in its ear.

The death of his mother left Arjun a sadder and a more matured boy. He was nearly fourteen and growing rapidly. The old schoolmaster had become greatly attached to his keen-minded, thoughtful young pupil, and frequently spoke of him as one who would bring honour to his house. Often when school was over, and the other boys had departed for their homes, these two would sit together at the school-house door, and the old man would tell tales of the great hot world beyond the mountains, or of Simla, and the fortunes which a persevering man might acquire there. And the boy would ask a thousand questions, which the teacher would try to answer, although he knew but little more than his pupil.

But there were other questions which Arjun did not ask the master, for, like all Orientals, he was

A PRIEST OF JACKO TEMPLE, NEAR KULU.

apt to conceal the things which lay closest to his heart. His mother's death, and the ceremonies attending, had raised doubts in his mind—stronger, appalling doubts which distressed him, and would not be dispelled. "Of course the Brahmins are holy, and the cow is holy; without their assistance, my mother's soul could never have gained Swarg (Heaven)," he would say to himself almost fiercely. But, just as he was assured that he had overcome the doubt, it would come creeping back again. "Thy mother was a good and faithful woman, serving her husband, caring for her children, and reverencing the gods; thy priest is noted for his greed and selfishness. He gains materially by his reverence of the gods; thy mother gained nothing material. She had none of his many faults. Then, if Swarg is the fruit of good deeds done in this birth, what had that priest, with his shloks, dough images and iron ladders, to do with thy mother's attaining it?"

One question gives rise to another, and before long the poor boy's mind was a maze of doubt. He no longer felt any confidence in the priests, or even in the gods whose ministers they professed to be. "They are all made of wood and silver and cloth and hair. Carpenters built them, and goldsmiths adorned them. If they wish to go anywhere they have to be carried, like my mother's coffin. The Pujaris (temple-priests) eat their food for them, and profess to give us answers in their name. Why, even a little babe can move, and eat, and make noises, and yet I never saw a god which seemed less helpless than a piece of common stone. How do I know that the greedy priests are not lying to us when they say that the spirits of the gods are in these things?"

Had Nihal Singh, or Brahmin Der, the priest, known the thoughts of the boy, they would have been much shocked. But he spoke of none of the things that were in his heart. Indeed, he was not much at home, for he had thrown himself into his studies with a whole-hearted zeal which delighted both his father and the schoolmaster.

By the time Arjun was sixteen he had completed the not very extensive course of studies offered by the little school at Khuni. The Sala strongly urged that the boy be sent to continue his studies at the Mission-school eight miles away on the other side of the ridge. "There he may read as far as the middle standard," said the old man. "He has a keen mind and loves to study. But give him the chance, and he will bring thee honour. With his spirit and the opportunity, he may yet be even a naib-tahsildar. These other boys—they are cattle; this school is enough for them. But Arjun thou must surely send over the ridge, and afterwards, if possible, to Simla."

"But it is a school of the Padri Log (missionaries)," objected Nihal Singh. "I like not the idea of sending him to a place so full of low-caste foreigners. I have heard that they seek to break our caste and make us as unclean as themselves."

"Fear not for thy son," the other replied. "He is a high-souled boy, worthy of his race, and will not have his head turned by anything so mean and low as a foreign faith. Trust him, and learn that I speak truth."

So it was decided that Arjun should begin to "read" at the Mission-school beyond the ridge in the following autumn.

IV.

A NEW SCHOOL.

On the morning of a bright day in the early autumn Nihal Singh and his son took the road for the Mission-school. On Arjun's back was a small kilta—the long basket, used only in the mountains—and in it were a brass dish, a little brass pot called lota, and a week's uncooked provisions—roughly ground flour, lentils, and a little clay pot of ghi. On top of the basket was a roll of mountain blankets.

The road from Zahu to the Mission-station is very beautiful. First it winds, rough and littered with stones, up to the top of the ridge. If you stand among the pines close to the little temple of Kali Mai you can get a commanding view of all that part of the country. Four or five hundred feet below lies Zahu, like a village of toy houses. From Bagi and Hattu, higher on the right, a great valley stretches away to the river Sutlej, on the distant left. Its sides are dotted with tiny

A MOUNTAIN BRIDGE ON THE WAY TO THE MISSION SCHOOL.

villages, fields of grain and stretches of forest. Down in the valley one can catch a glimpse of the roofs of the great temple of Karahan, and over the opposite ridge the Tibetan mountains stand out clear against the skyline, more than a hundred miles away.

Arjun, standing on the ridge, looked down at the village below as if he were never to see it again. As he hitched the kilta into position, and turned to follow his father, he somehow felt that he was leaving his childhood behind him, and that henceforth his life would be made up of stern duties, which he would have to meet as a man.

The road now led through forests of pine and cedar and mountain oak. Sometimes they followed its winding course, and sometimes leaving it, they travelled by short cuts which led for miles through damp leafy paths and brought them out upon the main road again, long after Arjun had come to the conclusion that they were hopelessly lost.

At length the road emerged from the forest, and after skirting a cultivated hillside for a mile or two dropped steeply down toward the Mission-station.

The Mission-schoolhouse is a two-storey building of stone. At one end is a large sleeping room, where those who live at a distance from the place are accustomed to spend the nights. For the Hindoos there is a kitchen also, and a high-caste cook, who prepares for the boys such provisions as they bring from home. In this way the requirements of caste are satisfied, and the boys are enabled to devote themselves to study.

Arjun felt himself at home almost immediately, as the "boarders" at the time were all Hindoos, and four or five of them were boys whom he had known at the Khuni school. Nihal Singh took him down to the house of the headmaster, a dapper little Indian with a kindly face, who wrote his name and age in the school register, and told him to be punctual and work hard. His father then bade him good-bye and started home; he did not wish to traverse that road through the woods after dark. "Even a Rajput cannot always overcome demons, and I have no desire to meet Sankra Bir on his white horse," he said to himself as he trudged up the slope.

Arjun went with one of the Khuni boys to look at the Mission-station, and was greatly interested in all that he saw. "What is that queer-looking house below the school, with another little house at one end of the roof?" he asked. "That? Why that is the girja (church), where the Christians worship their god," replied his companion. "Oh, I have heard of the Christians," said Arjun. "My father has told me that they are all low caste; that they have been untrue to the religion of their ancestors. They must indeed be evil people, and I shall avoid them as much as possible." "That thou canst not easily do," the other replied, "for every morning we all come to this girja, and sit while the Christians do their puja (worship), and at the close of school also they have a curious worship, in which they talk to their god, even as I now talk to thee."

"It is a great shame," said Arjun hotly, "that they should force us to be present at their puja. Were it not that I desire to gain knowledge, I should most certainly refuse to be present at any of their religious exercises." And he walked away abruptly, leaving his companion standing astonished in the road, "Of a truth," said the lad from Khuni to himself, "these Rajputs are all alike—proud and as impatient of restraint as the kings whose descendants they claim to be."

Arjun was up bright and early, and when the school-bell rang reported punctually in the big assembly room. The roll was called, and the boys forming into lines marched over to the church for morning prayers. Arjun marched in with them, his feelings divided between resentment and curiosity.

The first thing which he did after they were seated was to nudge his companion and ask, "Where is their god?" "They haven't got any," answered the boy, "or at least I never saw one, but I have only been here a few weeks myself." Arjun was astonished, and awaited developments with increasing interest.

The missionary in charge of the station was absent for a few days on a preaching tour, so the service was conducted by the schoolmaster. First they all stood up and sang something out of a little book. The tune was different from anything he had ever heard in the mountains, and seemed to him very queer indeed. The desire to be polite alone restrained him from bursting out laughing. Then followed the general confession and the rest of the service. Arjun could understand but little what was said, for the prayers were couched in terms with which he was utterly unfamiliar. But this much he grasped; that the Christians seemed to be trying to talk to their God, and that they addressed Him as a Father, loving and tenderly merciful.

THE MISSION SCHOOL TO WHICH ARJUN WENT ON LEAVING HIS FIRST SCHOCL.

"But where can it be that they keep him?" he asked himself again and again.

"I shall ask the headmaster on the first opportunity."

After the service the boys returned to the schoolroom, and began their studies. Arjun worked with the best of them, but several times he was unable to keep his thoughts from wandering off to the strange, outlandish puja which he had witnessed that morning. "They called him 'Father'!" he kept saying to himself. "Yes, 'Merciful Father' were the very words they used. Wah! who would ever think of calling Sankra Bir 'Merciful father'?" and he chuckled at the thought. "Our gods be all alike. They must be supplied with ghi (clarified butter) and their servants the pugaris made fat with gifts; year by year goats must be slain in their name, and we must dance before them at the melas, otherwise they will blight our crops and make our women childless. Merciful and loving! Why we dare not even go abroad at night, lest we meet them in field or jungle and they slay us. And these Christians call their god merciful! Of a truth it is a strange and outlandish idea."

A few days later the boy had an opportunity

to ask the headmaster about the whereabouts of the Christian's god. He was walking towards his home with some books under his arm, and Arjun offered to carry them. "Master ji," he ventured, "is it permitted to ask a question?" The man gave his assent, and the boy continued: "Morning by morning we all go to puja in the girja below the school. There many prayers are said before the god of the Christians. Mayhap the god dwells in the little house on the roof?" He meant the church tower. An English boy would have asked bluntly where the god was kept, but most Indians dislike direct questions.

Then the master took him to his home, and, sitting down, told him about the God of the Christians—the great eternal God, who made the heavens and the earth, and who "dwells not in temples made with hands". And he spoke of God's love for the poor, suffering human race, and of His plan for their salvation. He explained how the whole race of man, being too weak to overcome its animal nature, had fallen into impurity and loveless selfishness. "So we were all wandering in darkness, suffering the fruit of our evil deeds. God is perfectly holy, and our sins rose up like a wall, hiding Him from us, and preventing us from approaching Him. His holiness and our foulness could no more dwell together than can light and darkness. Yet we longed to worship, and since our sinfulness blinded our eyes so that we could not see and turn to the God who made us, we began to make gods for ourselves out of wood and stone and gold and silver, and somc of us bowed down to the forces of Nature, and the sun and the stars. Thus we tried to satisfy our longing, but we did not succeed, for we were groping about like lost travellers in the night of our own sinfulness. In every one's heart were unrest and anxiety and fear."

"I know that feeling," said Arjun ; "sometimes I get so tired and puzzled that I want to die. The world has little joy in it, and so very much sadness. My mother died last year."

"But God knew all about our troubles," continued the master. "And, because He loved us, He suffered in all our sufferings, and desired to save us from them. Now listen to the method He chose. Man had become so sinful and fleshly that he was conscious only of things that were fleshly and material. And since man could only understand the things of the flesh, God, in infinite condescension, purposed to manifest Himself to His poor blind children through the one thing they could at that time understand—the flesh. But how was He to do this? He ordained that a certain maiden should give birth to a child so spotless and free from the taint of sin that He could be one in holiness with God, His Father. And the child was born—a perfect and holy man, the only being in all the world with whom God might hold perfect communion. And from the moment of His birth God dwelt in Him in all the fulness of His Godhead, and was perfectly united with Him in holiness and love. Thus He who was born was perfect God, because God dwelt in Him in all His fulness, and also perfect man, because His humanity was real humanity. And being one with God in His divinity, and one with mankind in His humanity, He became the Way of our salvation. For we, being one with Him in our common humanity, were able through His spotless and holy humanity to enter into perfect communion with the Godhead, dwelling in Him. Therefore this being—perfect God and perfect man—has become the true Way whereby lost, groping man may pass out of the darkness into the light of the presence of God."

"And what is his name?" asked Arjun in an awed voice.

"One of His names," said the master, "is Im-

PRACTISING GYMNASTICS AT ARJUN'S SCHOOL.

manuel, which means 'God with us'. His other name is Jesus Christ, the son of man, and the Son of God."

"Tell me more about Him, Master ji," the boy begged.

The older man paused a moment, his head bowed in silent prayer, then continued: "Yes, He came to dwell among men—came poor and weak, that He might share all their burdens. He lived among us, humble, gentle, loving, healing the sick, cleansing the lepers, even raising the dead. For curses He gave blessings, and prayed for the poor deluded men who sought to kill Him. At last He suffered Himself to be slain, that even in undergoing death He might share to the full the burden of the human race."

"He died then?" faltered Arjun. "But can God die?"

V.

HE BEGINS TO DOUBT.

"HE died then?" faltered Arjun. "But can God die?"

"No, my boy, God cannot die. They slew the body of Jesus upon the cross, and that part of His nature which He shared with humanity died there even as all men die. But because the sinless humanity of Jesus Christ was perfectly linked with His deathless divinity, it pleased God to raise that slain humanity to life again, and join it to Himself with an eternal union, Jesus Christ. And after His resurrection, He appeared to those who had loved and followed and believed in Him, and for forty days He associated with them freely, eating their food and allowing them to touch Him. During this period He taught them, and told them that all power in heaven and on earth had been given to Him. Moreover, He ordered His followers to go into all the world and teach all nations, baptising them in the name of the Father, and of the Son, and of the Holy Ghost. This command and these names I cannot at present explain to thee, but I shall give thee the story of His life, as it was written by those who knew Him while He was in the world.

"However, when He had taught them all things, He led them to a hillside at some distance from the city where they were staying at the time, and even while He was talking with them He was taken up, and a cloud received Him out of their sight. And while they were looking steadfastly into heaven, as He went, two men in white appeared standing by them, who said to them, 'Ye men of Galilee'—they were natives of a country of this name—'why stand ye gazing up into heaven? This Jesus, who is taken up from you into heaven, shall so come in like manner as ye have seen Him go into heaven.'

"And while He dwelt among men He taught His followers many things, all of which are written in the little book which I am about to give thee. 'I am the light of the world,' He said; 'He who follows Me shall not walk in darkness, but shall have the light of life.' And we Christians believe that those who have faith in Him, and love Him and obey His commandments, shall find rest and joy in Him, and finally shall, by His grace, become like Him, and, after this earthly life is ended, dwell with Him in a life which has no end."

Arjun took the little book, and, thanking the master, walked thoughtfully away—not to the schoolhouse, but out into the woods, where he could sit down by himself and think over the strange new things which he had just heard.

How different it all was from what he had always been told was religion! Here were no petty godlets, ready to slay those who angered them, and hungry for sacrifices. Here were no greedy priests, giving little and asking much. A god who loved, and wished to help men! It was a glorious idea. "If I only knew that it were true, nothing could keep me from becoming a Christian," he said to himself.

He opened the little New Testament at random and began to read, "Come unto Me, all ye that labour and are heavy laden, and I will give you rest. Take My yoke upon you, and learn of Me; for I am meek and lowly of heart; and ye shall find rest unto your souls. For My yoke is easy and My burden is light."

SIPI IDOL AND PRIEST, WITH SACRIFICIAL KNIFE, NEAR KULU.

"Oh, if it were only true!" He closed the book and rose with a tired little sigh. "That is what I long for—rest and a reason for living." And he walked slowly back to the schoolhouse.

To us who were born in a Christian land, it may seem strange that a boy not yet seventeen and so full of life should long for rest. But India is full of such to-day—boys and young men with a soul-hunger which the religions of their fathers are not able to satisfy. It is this very hunger which has given rise to so many of the reforming sects which have sprung up there during the last quarter of a century.

Arjun's experiences during the next few weeks were many and varied. The little town in which the school was situated seemed a very city to the boy, who had never seen a village of more than twenty-five houses before. There was a little bazaar, and a number of the traders who kept shops in it were from the plains. These men greatly interested Arjun, and the tales they told of life in Amballa and Lahore opened up a new field of speculation for him. The world beyond the mountains became a reality to him, and it began to dawn upon him that Zahu was not the centre and pivot of the universe.

About this time, also, the boy had an opportunity to see something of the "Sahib boy," about whom he had heard so much. It was on a Saturday afternoon, and he was on the road to his home in company with two of the lads from Khuni. They were trudging along together, happy in the anticipation of a week-end at home, when suddenly, at a turn in the road, they encountered a long line of coolies. They carried leather-covered boxes, tents, folding beds, bedding, hampers, and a variety of other things which the boys had never seen or even heard of before.

"It must be a Sahib!" cried one of the lads in excitement. "Let us climb up on the bank and watch him go by." The three clambered up above the road, and stood eagerly waiting. Arjun was keenly interested; he had heard many stories of the queer foreigners who wore strange outlandish clothes and put their waist-coats on under their coats, instead of over them like ordinary people. He had been told by his father that they were a nation of crazy men, who did things without any rhyme or reason. "I myself once went with one of them ten days into the interior, and would you believe it, he did nothing but climb to the top of a mountain, and then climb down again and come back!"

In a few minutes the party swung round the corner, and passed below the place where the lads were standing. It consisted of three young Englishmen, dressed for a holiday, and probably on their way into Kulu to shoot bears. They were entirely unconscious of the three silent little mountaineers on the bank above them.

When they had passed the boys took the road again. "What a funny-looking crowd they were!" said one of the Khuni lads. "Did you ever see such clothes or hats?" and he laughed. "Or such faces," joined in another. "Why, they looked as if they had been boiled. And their hair was such an ugly colour—just like straw!" "There is a cat in Zahu, and its eyes are just the colour of the eyes of these sahibs," observed Arjun. "I wonder if they mind looking like that?" There was a touch of pity in his voice. "I don't believe so," said the oldest boy. "They probably get so used to it that they do not even notice it."

Arjun spent the week-end with his father and little sister. Nihal Singh seemed well pleased with the progress which his son was making and gave him much advice as to how he should conduct himself. "Remember," said he, when bidding his son good-bye, "thou goest back to study, and to learn *all* that thy masters can teach thee. I look to thee to be a credit to thy house. Be willing, polite and obedient. Above all, have nothing whatever to do with the religion of the Christians. To go to the girja thou must, for this is the order, but when there think of thy studies, and pay no heed to what the Padri says or reads out of the Christian's book. I have known men who foolishly listened to the words of that book, and later went to the bad, in fact became Christians themselves, and dishonoured their families and their villages. So be careful and remember who thou art."

So far as his study was concerned, the boy strictly followed his father's advice. Over and over again he won the praise of his teachers for the neatness of his work, and the ability with which it was executed. He was courteous also and obedient. Moreover, led by a desire to comply with his father's wishes, he put the little book which his master had given him at the bottom of his box of belongings, and resolved not to read it, for the present at least.

But in one thing he found himself utterly unable to obey. Try as he would to think of his studies only, the morning devotions in the girja gripped his attention with a power impossible to

HOUSES IN THE VILLAGE WHERE ARJUN LIVED.

describe. Day by day he would march in with the other boys, firmly resolved to think of his lessons, but before many minutes had passed he would be listening to the service with breathless intensity. Often and often too, as he was playing with the other boys, the words which he had heard in the morning would keep running in his ears.

There was something which touched him infinitely in the way the Christians, kneeling together, with one voice confessed to their "Almighty and most merciful Father" that they had been weak and sinful, straying from His ways like lost sheep. On such occasions the unsatisfied hunger of his soul would resolve itself into a longing to know some god whom he might call "Heavenly Father"—a god to whom he might bring all his perplexities, and in whom he might find the rest for which his soul was longing. Thus he would remain throughout the service, conscious not so much of the words as of the emotions and longings that the whole atmosphere of the place kindled within him. But when the boys had come out of the church and the hum of study began to be heard again, his mind would be drawn back to the things about him, and he would remember his reason for coming to the

Mission-school, and his father's parting words. Then he would bitterly reproach himself for allowing the service to influence him, and would make a firm resolve to keep his mind distracted on the morrow.

VI.

GHOST STORIES.

THE weeks passed and autumn gave place to winter. Then the kitchen became the most popular place. There the boys ate their meals and prepared their lessons, while Sita Ram cooked, and the wood-fire filled the room with warm light and shadows. There also on Friday and Saturday nights, when the week's work was ended, they would sit and tell each other the stories which they had learned while children at home. At these times Sita Ram, the cook, was in his element, and as he wandered from one tale of ghosts and vampires to another, the boys would huddle closer together, glancing nervously at the door and the dark corners of the room, as if they half expected some fearful visitant to drop in upon them.

"Heard ye ever of how the jhous once took to devastating Komarsen?" he asked them one evening. None of the boys knew the story, and they gathered around him expectantly. "Some years ago," he began, looking at his hearers impressively, "it came about in Komarsen that one of the people died every eighth day, and the whole village was greatly distressed. They tried in many ways to learn the cause. The god of the place at first refused to enlighten them, and all their gifts seem to have been wasted. Becoming more and more desperate, however, as the number of the dead continued to increase, they renewed their supplications, and gave many gifts to the priests. At length the god revealed to one of his garnetos (a devotee through whom a god voices his wishes) that the deaths in the village were caused by jhous (vampires), who had leagued themselves together against the community. This news filled the people with consternation, almost amounting to despair. The Brahmins were unable to do anything, and the villagers continued to die. Now at that time there was a young man in Komarsen, famed for his uprightness and for his knowledge of charms and magic. This youth resolved, if possible, to free his neighbours from the ravages of the jhous.

"On the next eighth day a man died as usual, and was taken out to the burning-place. When the torch had been applied and the people had

A BUDDHIST TEMPLE NEAR WHERE ARJUN LIVED.

departed to their homes the young man approached the spot alone and built him a tiny hut close to the burning pyre. Then he seated himself in it and waited.

"Just at midnight he saw a jhou come out of the ground close by the still smoking fire, and then another, and another, until there were a great number standing about the fire. And among them he saw those who had been dying in the village. Last of all came up the jhou of the man whose body had just been burned. And they looked at each other and licked their lips, saying, 'Aha! what a nice fat one there was this time!'

"There is a very powerful charm, called karkundli, made with the name of Maha Dev and many other great gods. The man who knows this charm can, by repeating it at the proper time, bind the jhous, so that they will be unable to move either hand or foot without his leave. So the young man sitting in his hut began very quietly to say the karkundli, and continued until all the jhous about the fire stood motionless and unable to depart. And thus they remained all night, he sitting in his hut repeating the magic words, and they standing motionless about the pyre.

"Now a jhou can by no means endure the light of day, and as they saw the first faint flush of dawn above the eastern hills, the spirits began to implore the young man to let them go.

"'Not until you promise to cease from killing the people of my village,' he answered. For a long time they stood silent, but at last, as the sky above began to lighten, they promised. Thereupon he repeated the words which would free them, and they disappeared.

"Thus was Komarsen saved from the ravages of the jhous. Should not I know, whose mother's sister married a man of the place?" and he looked at the boys, nodding solemnly.

"What are jhous exactly?" Arjun asked the cook.

"All people have to live their lives in pairs," answered Sita Ram. "First there is a life among living people—as we live now. Then there is a life to be lived among the jam log (the dead). When we have died we will become jhous, and we will live with the jam log."

"But how say the Brahmins that the soul goes to heaven or hell to reap the fruit of the deeds done in this life?" persisted the boy. "I never heard them say that we had first to lead another life."

THE ROAD FROM ZAHU TO THE MISSION SCHOOL TO WHICH ARJUN WENT ON LEAVING HIS FIRST SCHOOL. THIS SHOWS THE WILD COUNTRY IN WHICH THE VILLAGE OF ZAHU IS SITUATED.

"That does not make it any less true that there are jam log," said the cook. "The Brahmins do not know everything. And it is only natural that they should forget the spirit life when it brings them no profits." Like all hillmen the cook liked to laugh at the greed of the Brahmins, but he would have been the last to do anything without consulting them. "The truth of the matter is this—that after a man has lived and died his pair of lives, he goes to heaven or hell to reap the fruit of them," he concluded.

"But do the jam log always try to injure the people who live in the world?"

The cook answered in the affirmative.

"Then I don't believe in them," said Arjun. "The priests perform the rites which make it possible for our souls to enter heaven, and that we may safely pass Batherni a cow is given. It is foolish to think that all—even good men—*must* live another life, worse than the one they lived in the world."

"Believe in them or not, as it pleases thee," retorted Sita Ram in a vexed tone. "Thou canst not make it false by not believing. We have a most sure proof that there are jam log. Hast ever heard of the jam-tal? No? It is kept by the priests in the temple at Komarsen, and they came by it thus.

"There was a man of Komarsen travelling along a road one night alone. As he was walking through some woods in great fear, he came to a clearing, and there he saw five or six jhous sitting on the ground and eating out of a great gold dish. The jam log at once asked him to sit down, purposing to kill him after their repast was ended. All at once something must have occurred in the spirit-world, for the jhous began to gaze fixedly all in one direction. And the man, when he saw that they were taking no notice, jumped up, and, seizing the jam-tal (the dish of the dead), ran for his life. The jhous saw him making off down the road and pursued him, but he reached Komarsen before they were able to seize him, and gave the gold dish to the priests, who hid it in the temple, where no jhou is able to enter. Three days later the man died. There, is that not proof that there are jam log?"

"Did you ever see that gold dish, cook?" asked the lad.

"No," answered Sita Ram, "but the Brahmins there have told me all about it. They say that the jam log might injure me if they knew that we had seen their jam-tal."

Arjun asked no more questions. "Lying priests and superstitious people," he reflected bitterly. "Poor chance have we of learning the truth from such!"

The spiritual experiences of the last two months had given the boy a keenness of perception which made him quick to detect flaws in the rough legends of the mountains. The truth was battering at the door of his heart, and although he was doing his best to resist it, he had not been able to shut out all the light. Consequently he looked at the things which he had believed implicitly two years before with the eyes of a new understanding, and marvelled at himself for having ever thought them true.

VII.

KARTHAR SINGH APPEARS.

THE snow cleared away at last, and with the spring there came a young man from the plains to be a guest of the headmaster. The boys were very much interested in the stranger, and many were the questions which they asked each other about him. Who was he? Where was his home? Why did one who showed by every word and look that he was of Hindoo extraction eat with a Christian and treat him as an equal? And when it became rumoured about that he was the son of high-caste and wealthy parents, he became an even greater object of interest to the boys than before.

One day he accompanied the master to school, and, after the day's work was completed, lingered at the place and got into conversation with one of the boys. In a few minutes they were joined by a number of others interested to learn what they could about the newcomer.

A MOUNTAIN SHEPHERD CARRYING A LAMB IN HIS BOSOM.

A SHIVITE HILL TEMPLE, NEAR KOTGURH.

Arjun was not among them, but the stranger was the principal subject of conversation at the evening meal, and he soon was acquainted with what the boys had been able to learn. To be sure it was not very much, but it kindled in him a great desire to talk with the master's guest and learn his story from his own lips.

"Well, I think that he has sinned a great sin," said Narain Das, the son of one of the Brahmins of the place. "If he was born a Sikh, of high caste and good family, what right had he to defile himself by becoming a Christian?"

"So say I," added another. "Whatever he may have thought, he had no right to bring dishonour upon his family. Had he been my son, I would have beaten him well, until he had come to his senses."

"But that is what they did do," said one of the boys from Khuni. "I gathered from what he told us that they had punished him not once but many times."

"He is telling us the truth," said one of the most thoughtful; "of that I am sure. But the thing which puzzles me is, What had he to gain by the step? He is not the first of whom I have heard who gave up worldly prospects, home and caste to throw in his lot with the sweepers and leather-workers who have become Christians. Apparently they have had everything to lose and nothing to gain."

"That is the very question which has been puzzling me," said Arjun, and he determined to have a talk with the stranger and find what his answer would be to it.

Not many days had passed when the desired opportunity came. Work was over, and Arjun had gone out into the woods to study one of his next day's lessons. He had not been long there when he heard a footstep on the road below him, and looking down saw the young guest of the schoolmaster walking quietly along. His head was bowed as if in thought, and he had a little book in his hand.

The boy hastily put his reader into his pocket, and scrambled down to the road. The other saw him coming, and waited, greeting him with a kindly word and a smile which at once banished any shyness which might have been troubling him.

"Salam ji" (Greeting, sir), he began. "Have you any leisure at this time? and, if so, may I walk with you for a little way?"

The other gladly assented, and they walked along the shady path winding among the pine-

SIKH SADHUS (HOLY MEN).

trees, and entered upon a conversation which was destined to change the whole course of Arjun's life.

"Have I your permission to ask a question?" asked the boy earnestly.

"Gladly," said his friend; "ask all you desire, and, as far as I have power to do so, I will answer."

"Tell me how it happened that you have become a Christian," Arjun asked. "They tell me that you were a Hindoo—a Mangat Sikh—and that you left everything to throw in your lot with the Christians. What made you do this?"

"Yes, I will tell you all about it," replied his companion; "but let us first find a quiet place where we can sit and talk without fear of interruption. It will be easier for me to tell you everything if we are alone."

Arjun knew of a quiet spot a short distance away, and led his new friend there. When they were seated, and safe from fear of interruption, the young convert began:—

"My honoured father is a lambardar (headman) of Rampur, in the plains. He has four sons, of whom I am the youngest, being the child of his old age. Probably this was the reason why he loved me most of all.

"They say that even when I was a little boy I was of a religious disposition, and was never so happy as when accompanying my father to the Ghurdwara, or taking part in the household worship.

"As soon as I was old enough to go, my father sent me to the village school. There I learned to read, and first came in contact with the Bible of the Christians. The school was carried on by missionaries, and when first they told me that I must read the Bible I left the place. Afterwards, being anxious to learn English, I returned to them, and submitted to the Bible instruction.

"At first I read everything with a rebellious heart, hating the good things which they taught me because I thought them Christian ; but as time went on I began to look forward to the lessons, and to hear of Jesus with a softened heart. Thus for several years I learned and grew, and I came to admire the Gospels and the teaching of Jesus, looking upon Him as a great religious teacher, as our own Guru Nanah Sahib.

"I cannot tell how the change came, but one day Jesus became alive and real to my soul. He was no longer a dead teacher of beautiful truths, but my own dear, living, loving Lord. Do not ask me how this came about, for I do not know.

All that I can say is that before I had only known *of* Him! from then on I knew *Him.* He took my heart by storm, and became the satisfaction of all my wants and the centre of all my life.

"I remember with what joy the consciousness of His presence filled me, and with what great thankfulness I rose to follow Him. When first I told my people that I must serve Christ they laughed at me, and thought to turn me from my purpose by telling me that if I ever did anything so foolish I would become a companion of sweepers and chamars (leather-workers). From this they proceeded to abuse, and at last to violence, hoping thus to weaken me. Hardest of all, my mother who bare me would come to me, begging me with tears not to leave her childless in her old age, and my father's face grew thin and anxious.

"Over and over again I would feel the weight of the Cross I had taken up; and as I saw the sorrow of those who loved me, and the shadow over the home where I had spent my boyhood so happily, the desire would sometimes come to give up my purpose, and conform to the wishes of my people.

"But Christ never allowed me to forsake Him. He had bound me to Himself with bonds of a love before which everything else had to give way. And when I thought to leave Him, He told my soul that I could not—that I had begun to live in Him, and could not live apart from Him.

"When I was seventeen I cut off my long hair. It was the badge by which a Sikh was known, and I did not feel that I could wear it. It was this act of mine which brought matters to a crisis. There was a woman in our house—the wife of my oldest brother. She was a very worldly woman, and hated me because she feared that I was about to bring dishonour and shame upon the family. When she saw that I could by no means be turned from my purpose of following Christ, she determined to prevent me from bringing disgrace upon the house by taking my life. She watched her opportunity, and when she thought the time was ripe placed some poison in my food.

"I ate the food, and nearly died, being in the greatest torture for a day and a night. I shall never forget the agony which I suffered while the poison was working in my body, but I am thankful that it was so great, for it was then that I tasted the joy which comes to those who suffer for Jesus, and I seemed to hear a voice within my heart comforting me, and to feel a hand on my brow giving me strength.

"As soon as I had somewhat recovered, and was able to walk about, I decided that it would be best for me to leave my home. There was a Mission station not many miles away, and I made my way thither. The poison had weakened me very much, and I was a long time on the road. When I reached the Mission, exhausted and ready to faint, the missionaries received me and cared for me lovingly. I told them how Christ had called me, and how I had given myself to Him. When they had heard all my story they received me as a brother, arranging for my food and lodging, and giving me daily instruction in the truths of the religion of Christ.

"I had been there scarcely a week when my people learned of my whereabouts, and made an attempt to take me away from the Station. They came into the grounds of the Mission, and with them about a hundred of their fellow-castemen, armed with long bamboo poles and other weapons.

"First they went to the house of the missionary in charge of the Station and demanded that he should give me up. 'I cannot do so,' he replied. 'I have neither the power to keep him here, nor to surrender him to you. He is old enough to choose for himself, and the law gives him a right to do so. We will call him, and he shall decide for himself whether he wishes to remain here or go back with you to Rampur.'

"I was rather nervous when they called me into the room. There had always been a very close bond between my father and me, his youngest son, and it was very hard to see him in tears, and hear him pleading for me not to disgrace my family by breaking caste. He spoke of his own sorrow, and dwelt on the distress of my mother, who was broken-hearted at the step I had taken.

"My poor father's face was thin and haggard, and eloquently witnessed to the truth of his words. And when at last he stretched out his arms and implored me brokenly to come home and make them all happy again, I could hardly resist the longing to do so, for I loved my people. One thing alone held me back; I knew my family, and I knew that if I returned to them it must be as a Sikh. The choice lay clearly before me—to give up Christ for my people's sake, or to give up my people for Christ's sake. I thank God that He gave me the strength to choose Christ.

"At length, when they learned that I could

CAMEL CART, N.W. INDIA.

neither be moved by fear nor love to give up my purpose, they went away, taking my father with them.

"Since then I have been reading and studying, in the hope that some day Christ may use me. Two months ago I graduated from the Punjaub University, and came up here this summer in order to have some weeks of quiet study before going to the Theological School."

He was silent, and neither spoke for some moments.

"Have you ever regretted your action?" asked Arjun at last.

"No," replied the other, "never for a moment. My only regret is that I had not more to give up for Christ's sake."

"Do you not think that you should have stayed with your people? They loved you," was the next question.

"I think not," replied the young convert quietly. "My people need Christ too, and unless I myself come to Him I cannot hope to lead them to Him. Now that I am Christ's, I can pray with the hope that my prayers will be answered, and my chief prayer is that my family may find life in Christ."

"I have only one more question to ask," said

Arjun. "In the Gospel of the life of Jesus Christ I read some time ago an invitation, given by Christ to all who were tired and heavy-laden. His words were 'Come unto Me, and you shall find rest for your souls'. Tell me—what has Christ given you?"

All the boy's soul was in the question, and the other, catching the tone of suppressed earnestness in his voice, knew that he was talking to one who needed that which only Christ could give.

"Little brother," he said, and his voice shook with feeling, "Jesus Christ has given me all, and more than all, that He promised. My soul was hungry, and He satisfied it with Himself. As soon as I received Him, I knew that I had previously been unhappy because I had not possessed Him. Truly He has shown me that a man may have nothing beside Jesus, and yet be very rich."

. . . .

That night, in a room of the schoolmaster's house, a young convert from the Sikhs was pleading with God for the soul of a boy; and the boy, on his knees at the back of the schoolhouse, was dedicating his young life to God in Jesus Christ.

VIII.

ARJUN RUNS AWAY.

As we have said before, Arjun was a Rajput by caste, and therefore a member of the bravest and staunchest race in India. His people had been for centuries the kings and warriors of the land, and their history abounded in stories of battles and sieges in which Rajputs had died to a man, rather than surrender themselves to the enemy.

And thus it was that Arjun took up the Cross of his Lord as a little soldier, determined, by the grace of God, to serve Him to the end, and if need be to lay down his life for Him as readily as his ancestors had laid down theirs for the Rajas of Bushahr.

He could not be satisfied with half-measures. He had sworn allegiance to Christ, and he wished that all men should know it. Accordingly he amazed the boys, assembled in the cook-house for breakfast on the following morning, by calmly announcing that he was going to become a Christian.

His statement at first met with nothing but laughter. "Arjun, a Christian!"—the idea was delicious, and they enjoyed the joke immensely. But the boy, with a few earnest words, quickly brought their laughter to an end, and as they heard him quietly asserting his faith in Jesus Christ, and his intention to follow Him, their amusement gave way to dismayed astonishment.

By noon the news had reached Zahu, and Nihal Singh, his heart torn between anger and anxiety, was taking the road for Kotgurh.

Arjun knew that the words which he had spoken to his companions must soon reach his father's ears; he was therefore not surprised when Nihal Singh made his appearance.

He looked at the boy sternly. "Put on thy shoes, and come with me," he said; "I wish to have a talk with thee."

Arjun obeyed, but it must be confessed that his heart was beating very loudly as he followed the Rajput along the shady path and into the woods. He was feeling miserable too. It was the first time that he had ever felt a gulf opening between himself and the father whom he loved.

Nihal Singh had often been stern and severe with his son, but he had truly loved him, and the bond which bound the two together was very real and deep. It distressed the boy greatly therefore to think that he must now refuse to conform to the wishes of his father, and he nearly burst into tears as he followed him through the woods.

They walked along in silence until they came to a quiet place where no one would be likely to disturb them; then the Rajput turned on his son:—

"What is this nonsense which thou hast been chattering to thy schoolfellows?" he asked, and eyed the boy fiercely. "Well I know that thou wouldst never bring such shame upon thy caste as to leave it, but how didst thou so far forget thyself as to utter words so unbefitting a son of mine? I sent thee here to study, not to talk foolishness."

He looked at Arjun, as though expecting a reply, but receiving none continued:—

"My first thought, when the report of thy words reached me, was to take thee from the school, and set thee to minding goats again. But on further consideration I saw that thy talk this morning could be nothing but a boyish and unseemly jest, and so I have decided to let thee continue thy studies upon one condition." He paused for a moment, and then proceeded, watching his son's face narrowly the while: "First, thou must promise me that thou wilt have nothing to do with the religion of the Christians in the future; second, thou must come back with me to the school, and tell thy comrades that what thou didst say this morning was only a joke. Art thou ready to do this?"

Arjun did not answer, and his father's face grew dark.

"Arjun," he said, and his voice was low and fierce, "thou art my son, and I love thee. But if I thought that thou wouldst ever become a shame to thy house, I would kill thee here in the woods."

"Dost thou know," he continued, in a voice trembling with indignation and disgust, "dost thou know what Christians are—a crowd of beef-eating low-castes and sweepers. Art thou so lost to all decency as to wish to join thyself to such? And then hast thou realised what would happen if thou wert to take such a step? Thy relations and friends would loathe and despise thee, thy home would be closed to thee, and nothing would remain for thee but to leave all those whom thou dost love, and cast in thy lot with strangers and foreigners. Wheresoever thou shouldst go, all

THE MOUNTAIN VILLAGE WHERE ARJUN WAS BORN

men of respectable caste would look upon thee as an unclean thing, and would carefully guard their food and water from the pollution of thy touch."

Still Arjun was silent.

"Hast thou no answer for me, shameless one?" cried his father, at last losing all control of himself. "Wilt thou promise, or must I take thee home in disgrace?"

"It is better that I should go home with you," answered Arjun, "for I cannot promise what you ask."

"Then home thou shalt come, faithless boy," exclaimed Nihal Singh savagely, "and I warrant that we shall find means of bringing thee to thy senses before many days have passed!"

Late that night the Rajput returned to his home, and with him went his son, tired in body, but determined, by God's grace, to prove himself a true soldier and servant of Jesus Christ.

. . . .

Months passed and Arjun's schoolmates gradually ceased to miss their friend. The many interests of daily life claimed their attention, and they almost forgot the strange conduct of the young Rajput. Examination time came with all its hopes and fears. Old boys left and new ones came to take their places; new friendships were formed and old ones broken. Indeed, before summer had given place to autumn, and autumn to winter, the boy may be said to have passed entirely out of the thoughts and the lives of his schoolfellows.

But there was one who could not forget the bright-faced, earnest little mountaineer—one who had himself suffered, and forsaken all for the sake of Jesus. It was the young Sikh convert, the story of whose life had so interested Arjun. Who could know better than he the sufferings which awaited the Hindoo boy who dared profess his love for Christ? For long hours he would lie awake at night, thinking of the lad, and praying that God would look after him, and guard and strengthen him to be true to his Saviour. "Oh, loving Father!" he would exclaim in an agony of anxious love, "be with my little brother—Thy little son—in this hour of trial. He has dared the hate of the world for Thy sweet sake; be Thou his support now, for Thou alone canst be his help. He is so little, and the forces of darkness arrayed against him are so powerful! Oh, Jesus, wrap him in Thy loving arms and bear him safely through this 'valley of the shadow'!" Thus night after night he commended the boy to God's care as he lay sleepless on his bed, or paced his room in painful intercession.

One night he was entirely unable to apply himself to his books. Never before had he felt so deeply conscious of the burden of his little brother's sufferings. He turned from volume to volume, trying to find something which would fix his attention, but without effect. At length he rose, and putting out the light betook himself to prayer.

It was a night in the late autumn, cold and still. The ground outside was frozen and hard, but no snow had fallen as yet. A splendid full moon was bathing all the place with silvery light, and its rays poured in through the little window and over the kneeling form of the young man. But he was unconscious of the light, forgetful of the lateness of the hour. Down upon his knees at the feet of his Master he was pleading for the guidance of his little friend. He did not see the small figure approaching his house along the white road in the moonlight, or hear the first timid knock at the door. A second knock, louder than the first, aroused him. He stumbled to his feet and opened the door, to find Arjun standing before him.

For a moment he stood in wonder gazing at

him. He noted the weary droop of his shoulders and the dark circles beneath his eyes. Poor, tired little boy! At the thought of all that he must have suffered, a great pity seized the man, and he gathered him up into his arms as if he had been a little child. Tenderly he bore him into the house, and sitting down clasped him close to his heart. With a tired little sigh of content Arjun laid his head on the shoulder of his friend, and seemed about to give way to his weariness. Indeed the other thought that he had fallen asleep, when suddenly he started up, and peered about him with frightened eyes. "Oh, brother!" he exclaimed, in a voice ringing with anxiety and nervousness, "I must not think of resting now; I must leave here at once. If I am not far away before the day breaks, I shall be recognised and taken back to Zahu. I beg you not to ask me to rest; half the village will be here by noon to-morrow looking for me. I am very tired, and so nervous that I cannot think. Oh, please tell me what to do! It was very hard to get even here to you, but I knew that you, too, had been beaten, and starved, and worried day and night for Christ's sake, and so I was sure you would help me. I—I was"—and the boy broke down entirely, sobbing and trembling.

"COLD WATER FOR EVERY MEN." SUPPLYING TRAVELLERS WITH WATER ON THE ROAD TO SIMLA.

Whose heart would not have been touched by such an appeal? The man was deeply moved. Himself a convert, he was well able to understand the situation. The boy had been subjected to months of that heartbreaking persecution to which Hindooism condemns those who strive to escape from her clutches. The young convert remembered how awful it had been in his own case, and his heart bled for the boy. He remembered his mother's tears, and the pathetic pleading of his old father. He called to mind how his fellow-castemen had hated him, and how even the lowest of the low had pointed the finger of scorn at him. He remembered how lonely he had been in those days, and how the feeling that he was thought to be the disgrace of his family weighed him down. And Arjun, too, had suffered all this; as he looked at the thin, tired face of the boy he could not doubt it. "He has stood his test like a little soldier of Jesus," he thought, "and now something has happened which has made him feel that he must leave all. Christ helping me I will help him to get safely away, and since he cannot go alone I will accompany him, and see him safe in the hands of Christian friends."

"Little brother," he said, and again he clasped

the boy in his strong arms, "not only will I show you what to do, but I shall go with you, and with God's help bring you to a place where you will be safe from all these dangers. We will start within half an hour, and until then you must lie down on my bed and rest, for we have a long, hard journey before us, and both your strength and mine will be taxed to the uttermost before we reach the end of it."

He spoke quietly yet firmly, and Arjun obeyed him at once, falling asleep almost as soon as his head touched the pillow.

Meanwhile his companion busied himself preparing for their journey. First he wrote a short note, and addressing it to the missionary in charge of the station left it on the table. Then he went into the little kitchen adjoining his bedroom, and lighting a fire set some milk to boil. Softly he came back on tiptoe to the place where the boy was lying, and knelt down at the side of the bed.

Presently he arose from his knees, gently awakened Arjun, and bringing him a bowl of warm, sweet milk, bade him to drink it and prepare for the road.

IX.

A JOURNEY BY NIGHT.

It was shortly after midnight when they left the house. As they stepped out into the silent moonlit road and turned their faces toward Narkanda, it seemed to Arjun that God was with them in a very special manner. The feeling that they were not alone took possession of him, and filled his heart with peace. The nervous, haunted feeling, which had been weighing him down for days, passed quite away, and with it half his weariness. It almost seemed as if the gentle hand of Christ had been laid upon him in silent benediction.

The name of Arjun's companion was Karthar Singh, which may be translated "The Lion who acts," and no one could have been truer to the name he bore. While unable to act he had devoted himself to prayer for his little friend, and now when the time came for him to undergo danger for his charge he was entirely ready.

No one could have known better than he the danger and difficulties which he might have to face in bringing the boy to safety. He knew that if they were captured before reaching Simla it would go hard with them—that he might even be called upon to lay down his life. He realised that Arjun might be unable to endure the long hard march of fifty miles which lay between them and their destination. He knew the difficulty and the importance of keeping ahead of the mail-runners, who might carry the news of their departure to Simla, and thus enable the members of Arjun's family living there to intercept them and prevent them from entering the place. There was a possibility that they would meet some of the boy's relatives on the road, or arouse the suspicion of the officers at the police-station in the way.

Karthar Singh recognised all this and much more as he crept away from the little house that night, yet it was with no fear or indecision that he took the road. He was one who had learned to cast all his cares upon his heavenly Father, and to walk through the valley of the shadow in simple trust, well knowing that God was with him. Arjun, looking up into his grave young face, saw that it was filled with a light which

TARA DEVI. AN IDOL BETWEEN KOTGURH AND SIMLA.

was not the light of the moon—the light of joyous consecration and firm resolve—and the boy's heart thrilled with a new consciousness of God's presence, and he forgot to look fearfully about him as they entered the dark shadows of the forest.

The road wound up and up, skirting a great hillside. Sometimes the trees grew so tall and close together as nearly to obscure the light, sometimes the path led them through silent moonlit glades or along the edge of rocky cliffs, from whence they could see the tiny mountain villages nestled among their fields far, far below them.

At about three in the morning the road took an abrupt turn to the left and brought them out upon the Narkanda ridge. The first thing which caught Arjun's eye was the signboard standing directly on the top of the ridge, one arm pointing toward Komarsen and the other toward Tibet. How like a cross it looked, there on the hilltop! The boy looked at it with awe, and felt that, through the rough pieces of wood, God was speaking to him and inviting him to the road of the Cross.

They left the ridge behind them with a sigh of relief. It made them feel safer to know that it stood behind them like a great wall separating them from the villages where they were known and were in the most danger.

"Can we not rest now for a while?" Arjun asked his companion after they had covered about eighteen miles. "Not at present," the other replied, "we must not think of resting until we have passed Koti Kohad, and, if possible, not until we have come to Bangari. The farther we get from your home, the less risk there is of meeting those who know you, and though the road will be hard and long, we must be prepared for both weariness and blistered feet, rather than by delaying put ourselves in danger of being captured and carried back to Zahu." The very idea of recapture made the boy shudder. He resettled his mountain-blanket upon his shoulder afresh, and quickened his pace, inwardly rebuking himself for having thought of rest.

They trudged on all morning, and toward three in the afternoon entered Bangari. Both were very tired; poor Arjun could hardly drag one foot after the other. It was the first time he had made so long a march, and, moreover, he had not left the Mission house fresh and strong, but worn out and exhausted by the

THE NARKANDA PASS NEAR KOTGURH.

escape from his village. Now as they drew close to Bangari it required all his Rajput grit and determination to keep him from sinking down by the road, and refusing to go farther. Indeed, why should we say "his Rajput grit"? this could never have sustained him. It was Christ, his Master, who strengthened him and kept him by the way—Jesus, who knew what it was to be weary and exhausted. Arjun had taken up the cross to be sure, but he had also found one to bear it with him and to refresh him when he was fainting beneath its burden.

The people of Bangari were not of a suspicious temperament, and they knew neither of the young men. When, therefore, Karthar Singh and his companion limped into the village sarai,[1] they were able to rest for two or three hours, unbothered by curious questions.

Arjun had no sooner entered the low-roofed, mud-walled room which had been assigned to them than he cast his blanket on the floor, and throwing himself upon it fell into the deep sleep of one who is utterly exhausted. "Poor lad!" thought his companion, "it will be a hard pull for him from here to Simla. I hope he will be able to hold out until we reach there." True

[1] The public inn of an Indian village.

Christian that he was, he did not even think of his own blistered, swollen feet and aching body.

From a little shop near at hand he brought some mustard oil, and after gently washing the feet of the sleeping boy, he began to rub them with it. Carefully he went over all the tired muscles, pressing here and pulling there, as only one skilled in the art of Indian massage knows how to do. By the time that feet and legs and tired body were rubbed down to his satisfaction it was growing dusk. "The cows will be coming in ; I shall be able to get some milk," he thought, and again limped off, this time to the village sweet-shop.

Before long he returned with the milk, all hot, and sweetened as Indians love it. . Arousing Arjun he made him drink, and when the boy had again closed his eyes he wrapped himself in his own blanket and was soon fast asleep.

It was long after nightfall when Arjun awoke with a start and sat bolt upright in the darkness, listening intently. The room adjoining the one in which they were staying had been occupied while he slept. He could hear a fire crackling merrily and the occasional clatter of a brass dish, from which he gathered that somebody's dinner was in the process of cooking. But it was not sounds such as these which had caused him to start up so quickly from his sleep. Such sounds would no more arouse a boy in India than the whistle of a steam-engine or the rumble of a passing tram-car would arouse his little English brother in London.

What aroused him then? It was the voices of the occupants of the next room. They were speaking in the dialect which was only used in Zahu and the villages near it, and the voice of one of the speakers he recognised at once. It was that of his uncle—his mother's brother—a man whose fierce and brutal nature had always inspired him with distrust and terror. He was the owner of several villages near Koti Kohad, and was considered by his neighbours a great man. No wonder that the boy trembled at the thought that only a thin wall of mud and wood separated him from such a person.

He limped stiffly to the door and peeped out. The starry sky was cloudless, and the light of the rising moon was just silvering the tree-tops at the back of the village. No one seemed to be moving about, and the distant bark of a dog was the only thing which broke the silence.

Quietly he tiptoed to the side of his companion and awoke him. "The next room is full of men from our village," he whispered close to his ear, "and one of them is my uncle, who would kill me far rather than see me become a Christian."

X.

A MINUTE TOO LATE.

THIS news was enough to chase any remaining sleep from Karthar Singh's eyes. He was on his feet in a moment, and not five more minutes had passed before two dark figures might have been seen creeping stealthily down the narrow village street toward the Simla road. Two or three times Arjun looked back fearfully, almost expecting to see the door open and the men of his village pour out in pursuit, headed by his uncle.

With a sigh of relief they found themselves on the main road again, and set their faces toward Simla, tired and aching in body, but deeply thankful to be safely out of Bangari. "How fortunate it was that the boy awakened," thought Karthar Singh as he trudged painfully along beneath the stars. "How true it is that He giveth His angels charge over us. We may sleep all unconscious of danger, but He that keepeth us will not slumber. Had we slept through until morning it would have been most difficult to get away undiscovered." With such thoughts of thankful love he trudged along, and his heart grew glad and his step light as he meditated upon the goodness of the Heavenly Father and all His tender care.

The rest of the journey was not eventful. Once during the latter part of the night there was a stir in the bushes above the road, and some heavy animal went crashing off among the trees. Arjun, whose boyhood had been spent in the midst of the mountains, was able to explain to his comrade that it was probably a bear.

It was late in the afternoon when they reached Simla, creeping along with great difficulty. Arjun was so worn out that he hardly noticed the thousand and one strange new sights which met him at every turn. The gorgeously dressed servants, all glittering with scarlet and gold braid, could not draw one glance of admiration from him, nor the strange foreigners on horseback, or swinging along in their rickshaws. All he could do was to set his teeth, and press on blindly after his companion, dully wondering when he would be able to lie down. Poor

AN INDIAN PERFORMER.

Karthar Singh himself was not in much better condition.

Slowly they made their way along the crowded wall, past the great Town Hall, and down into the native bazaar. The steep, muddy lane took them by various twists and turnings between the shops of sweetmeat sellers, provision and cloth merchants, rickshaw-stands and little mountain temples down to the farther end of the bazaar. Some distance beyond the last houses they came upon a little house nestling in the midst of a quiet garden. Passing through the gate they approached the front door and Karthar Singh knocked.

It was opened by an old man with a long white beard and a quiet face, which lighted up with pleasure as he saw who had knocked. "Why Karthar Singh, my son, it is a joy to see you again! Come in, come in! You know that my house is your home whenever you will give us the pleasure of your company." Thus talking he led them inside, and made them sit down. "How tired you look!" he exclaimed, "and your young companion seems hardly able to sit up. I must arrange a room for you." And he hastened out, calling for the cook to heat water for a bath.

"Come now, my sons," he called, and Arjun,

as he heard the kind old voice, felt that he had found another true friend and a place where he might rest secure for a time at least.

They went into the other room, and found two beds prepared. "There is hot water in the bath-room, so bath and get to bed at once," said their host. "I will bring you something to eat, and then see that nobody disturbs you."

"Now God be thanked!" exclaimed Karthar Singh, with a sigh of relief, as the door closed and left them alone in the quiet room. "Little brother, before sleep or bath or tea, shall we not kneel down and thank the Lord Jesus for being our Saviour in the road thus far, and pray Him to guard us still from all danger?" And never was prayer more earnest offered. Surely the tender heart of Jesus must have filled with joy as He listened to the trusting and thankful prayers of His children. Surely that tender heart which had broken so often over the ungratefulness and selfishness of those it loved must have been greatly comforted as He looked down upon those two young soldiers, who had chosen Him and His Cross and the hatred and contempt of the world, rather than the ease and pleasures and earthly honour which those who did not love Him were ready to give them.

How many of us forget what pain we give our Saviour when we forget Him, and what comforts we could be to Him, if we would only give Him our hearts as Arjun did and Karthar Singh! How much happier the world would be if every one should try to so live that he would be a comfort to Jesus. Remember, my reader, that He is very dependent upon you and upon me for comfort.

At last the bathing was finished, and the two young men, refreshed with their tea, had fallen off into the deep sleep of exhaustion. The warm light streamed in slender bars through the window-lattice, and the flies buzzed dreamily about in the subdued light. Slowly the shadows grew longer; the spots of sunlight crept from the centre of the floor to the wall, and up the wall toward the ceiling, and at last faded away. The dusk of evening gave place to the darkness of night, and still the two slept on, unmindful of the passing time and the possibility of danger near at hand. They were not mindful, but their Heavenly Father was. His guiding hand was over them, and we may be sure that many a kind angel watched beside them as they slept.

Let us now return for a minute to Zahu, and see what happened there after Arjun's departure.

Nihal Singh awoke in the morning to find that his boy was missing. For several hours he did not suspect the boy had left the village. "He has probably gone over to his uncle's house to see his cousin Bishan Singh," he thought. "Breakfast time will see him safely back again. Trust a boy to be on hand at meal-times." He smiled as he thought of his own boyhood, and taking his stick started down to the mill to see about some grain which he had given to the miller to grind. Some hours later he returned along the road to the village, fully expecting to find the boy at home. "I might as well stop on the way, and see if he is still loitering with Bishan Singh," he thought, and stopped at the house to inquire. There he learned with surprise that Arjun had not been seen. Bishan Singh was helping his father in the field, and knew nothing of his cousin's whereabouts.

"A plague on the boy!" exclaimed the father with vexation as he set out for home with hurried pace. "I send him to school, and he plays the fool; I keep him here, and he is no better! What can one do with such a lad? What has come over him? He used to be obedient and never gave any trouble. It's all this school business; a curse on the ambition which made me send him there!"

INDIAN COOLIES ON THE MARCH.

The Rajput arrived at home in a very bad humour, fully prepared to give his son a sound beating for the anxiety he had caused him. He was met with the news that nothing had been heard of the boy, and again left the house to search for him, with a look on his brow which boded no good for the truant. After an hour's unsuccessful inquiry the suspicion began to dawn upon him that Arjun had run away. Another hour's search turned the suspicion almost to a certainty, and he returned home cursing and fairly grinding his teeth with fury.

An hour later he was on the road to the Mission-station and more than half the men of Zahu were with him. That a boy from their village—and the son of a Rajput at that—might possibly become a Christian, was not simply a private matter to be settled by the father. Each man and woman and child in Zahu felt that the honour of the village was at stake, and every one was ready to do everything possible to prevent it. Had Nihal Singh been a much less important person in his village, he could still have counted upon the hearty assistance of every one in the place.

The party reached the Mission at about five in the evening. There they learned that, although no one had seen or heard anything of Arjun, Karthar Singh's rooms had been found empty, and he himself was nowhere to be found. While they were still in the midst of the excitement of this discovery, Arjun's uncle—he who had spent the night before in the room next to Karthar Singh and the boy in the Sarai at Bangari—arrived upon the scene. He heard with astonishment and anger of his nephew's disappearance; but when he learned that the young Sikh convert was also missing, he turned to one of his companions and inquired, "When we were leaving Bangari this morning, did not the keeper of the Sarai tell us of a young man and a boy, who had come in very tired in the afternoon and left some time during the night?"

This was the first definite news which they had been able to obtain, and the party from Zahu lost no time in acting upon it. Bread was cooked for the road, and within a very short time a large party of villagers were swinging up the road toward Narkanda at a rapid pace. The party was made up of Nihal Singh's relatives and fellow-villagers, and with them returned Arjun's uncle, who, in the desire to recapture his nephew, had quite forgotten the long tramp he had done already that day from Bangari.

They marched all night, pressing on with a speed which nothing but their mountain training could have made possible. Before nine o'clock they were over the ridge; by five in the morning they were at Bangari cooking breakfast, and at eleven o'clock in the morning they might have been seen standing in the Simla railway-station scanning the faces of those who were entering the train. Nor were they alone, for with them stood an Indian gentleman, whose keen, intellectual face and general manner marked him out as a wakil, or pleader. Many were the looks of curiosity cast at the group of rough hillmen by the passengers. But the stern, intent expression upon their faces prevented people from troubling them with questions.

One of the passengers was particularly interested in the silent, outlandish group. In fact he was so interested that he wrote about them in a letter to his brother far away in England. It is upon this letter that we shall depend for an account of the events of that morning. The heading is "Lahore, December 18, 190—," and it begins as follows:—

"My dear Fred,—As you will see from my heading we are down in the plains again. The trip to Simla was delightful. The cold, bracing air quite reminded me of home, and was a great contrast to the heavy, moist atmosphere down here in the plains.

"On the day we left Simla I saw a rather interesting affair. We were comfortably seated in our carriage, waiting for the train to start, when suddenly the station became half filled with people, whose strange, outlandish appearance at once aroused my curiosity. I learned upon inquiry that they were natives of Bushahr, a small mountain kingdom lying to the north-west of Simla, several days' journey away.

"Well, we were looking at them, when suddenly the whole crowd surged forward, with yells and (apparently) curses—they had been silent until then—and seemed to be attacking a group of Indians who were trying to enter the train. The whole place became filled with confusion at once. There was a great rushing about and calling for policemen, and at last some semblance of order was established.

"As I told you, I had in the first place been interested in the hillmen, and so strolled over. to see what all the excitement was about. The party attacked seemed to be made up of an old man a young man and a boy. As far as I could gather all the fuss was over the boy.

ONE OF ARJUN'S FELLOW-COUNTRYMEN, SHOWING THE WAY IN WHICH THE HAIR IS TIED.

A HILL LAD DRESSED FOR HIS WEDDING.

When I arrived I found that a big, fierce-looking mountaineer had gripped him by the arm, and seemed bent upon carrying him off by force. The boy was not dressed in the clothes of the hills, but his face was enough like that of the hillman to make me suspect that he must have been his son. The young man with whom the lad had come to the station seemed quite as determined that the boy should not be taken away. He was a splendid-looking young Indian, and stood up for (what he evidently thought to be) his rights like a hero in the face of the wild yelling crowd. However, things would have gone badly for the little party had not the police-officer arrived on the spot with a number of his men. He bundled off the whole party quick as a wink—to the police-station, I suppose. However, that is the last I saw of them. It was an exciting last impression of Simla. The boy was a fine-looking little chap, and did not at all seem inclined to leave his young companion for the other fellow. Though I do not know the rights of the case, all my sympathies were with the boy and his companions.

"Yours, in haste, J."

As my readers must have gathered from the above letter it was Arjun and Karthar

Singh who had attempted to enter the train, and it was the crowd of mountaineers from Zahu who met them in the station and tried to take the boy away. The station-master had seen that the crowd was growing more and more excited, and, fearing an uproar, had sent for the police. Thus it was that just at the moment when Karthar Singh was beginning to despair of the boy's safety, and the people from Zahu were thinking that their efforts were to be crowned with success, the police came hurrying up and took them all off to the police-station.

It was a new turn of affairs. Arjun and his companion were very thankful for it, as it gave them another chance to escape from the clutches of the villagers. Arjun's father and his uncle were fiercely angry at the interference of the law, and, as they walked along, cursed their bad luck, the government, the police, the station-master, and everything else that seemed to stand between them and their object. As to the other villagers, they followed in the rear, half angry and half afraid, with visions of disagreeable police investigations and fines to be paid for disorderly conduct.

The police sub-inspector took down the charge against Karthar Singh. He was accused of kidnapping Arjun, and was committed to gaol pending trial before the district judge. Then turning to the boy himself he said, "Now, my boy, go with your father, and show him by your conduct during the next few days that you did not wish to come away". Poor Arjun! He looked at his father, standing there with stern face, and at his uncle. He looked in the direction of Karthar Singh, about to be led off to the gaol. Poor boy! he had never been away from his home before, and the sight of so many new faces entirely upset him.

"Why do you hesitate?" said the sub-inspector, looking curiously at him. "Have you not caused your father enough trouble already? You have brought him all the way to Simla, and put him to shame before strangers."

Still Arjun stood silent and miserable before the officer; it was only when his father stepped forward to take him by the arm that he seemed to recover himself.

Shrinking away from his angry parent he turned piteously to the officer, and putting his two hands together in the Indian gesture of supplication, he said tremulously, "Oh, sir, I do not wish to go with my father; please do not make me go. Truly I am old enough to leave home if I wish to do so. Can I not go to gaol with Karthar Singh? Please do not send me away with these people ;" his lips were trembling and he could hardly keep back the tears.

The sub-inspector was surprised at the earnestness of the boy. "Have you any idea why he ran away?" he asked, turning to the father.

"Yes, your honour," the man replied fiercely. "I sent him to the school of the Christians, and they practised enchantment upon him. Within a year he was saying that he wished to become a Christian himself. Of course I took him home. We are Rajputs, and I could not see him bring shame upon his family. I thought he was coming to his senses again, and indeed I did my best to beat the madness out of him, but it seems that he was hiding his purpose in his heart all the time. One morning I went down to the mill to see about some grain which they were grinding for me. Before starting I had missed him, but I thought that he must have gone up to the village. It was not until late in the afternoon that it dawned upon me that the shameless one must have run away. We followed him to the school and thence to Simla, where we found him in the act of entering the train with that cursed Christian." The Rajput's face was red with

WOMEN OF ZAHU ENGAGED IN HUSKING RICE. THEY POUND THE RICE WITH THE LONG POLES WHICH THEY HOLD IN THEIR HANDS TILL THE GRAIN IS SEPARATED FROM THE HUSKS.

anger, and his flashing eyes and trembling voice boded little good to his son if he but fell into his hands.

"Yes," thought the inspector, scanning the lines of suffering in the face of the boy; "I'll wager that he tried his best 'to beat the madness out of him'. Poor little lad! I'm inclined to think he would be safer away from his relatives for a few days at least." He was an officer of long experience, and knew of cases where boys had been forced to go home with tragic results.

"Well, boy," he said, turning to Arjun, "I cannot let you go to gaol with your friend; that would be entirely contrary to the regulations; but, on the other hand, I cannot force you to go with your father if you insist that you would rather not do so. For until the case is tried he has not proved that he has a right to make you return home. Now which shall it be; will you go with your people, or shall I have you locked up in a room by yourself until your companion is tried?"

"Please lock me up, your honour," replied the boy earnestly, and as he spoke he heard his uncle cursing him beneath his breath. The man was a thoroughly bad lot, and Arjun knew that rather than have him break his caste, he would gladly put an end to him.

The inspector also had heard the curse, and felt all the surer that he was acting wisely in not turning the boy over to his people. He wrote the order, therefore, and Arjun was led off to a cell, there to await the day of the trial.

It was a bare little room with a loophole window in one side. There were no chairs or bed, but to a boy of the mountains this was no hardship. He had never sat on a chair in his life, and as to bed—the mountain gods were supposed to be angry with any one who should dare to sleep on one.

How quiet it was! Down in the streets below he could hear the noisy rush and clatter of the busy world, but it seemed far away and almost unreal to him as he sat there in the shadowy half-light of the little cell. It seemed almost a relief to be safely locked up for a few days, after all the weeks of anxiety and uncertainty. "For two days, anyhow, nothing can happen," he sighed contentedly, as he sat watching the sun-beams play on the opposite wall. "I wonder where Karthar Singh is. Perhaps his room is next this one;" the thought and the desire came to him to learn whether his friend were at all near him. "He might hear me if I should sing," said he to himself, and forthwith decided to try.

Putting his face close to the window he began in a low clear voice the beautiful old Hindoo hymn "Yishu Masih mero prán bachaya" (Jesus Christ has saved my soul). Slowly he sang the first two verses through, listening between each for a response, and was just about to start the third when he heard it coming quite clearly from the window next his own :—

> **The river is deep, and the boat is worn out,**
> **Jesus, He will take me over.**

"He is in the very next room," thought Arjun joyfully, and with his face as close to the opening as possible, he called to his friend in a low voice. "Is that you, Arjun?" came the reply. "How is it that you are here?"

"The sahib was going to send me away with my father," whispered Arjun. "I begged him not to do it, but to send me here instead. So he put me in here until you are tried. Tell me what to do."

"The only thing you must do is to tell the truth, little brother," the other replied. "Tell the judge that you are nearly sixteen years old, and that you wish to become a Christian. When he asks you why, tell him plainly the reason. If he tells you that you have the choice of going home, or coming with me, answer him boldly that you wish to come with me. Under God, everything depends upon you now. Think about Peter who denied his Lord through fear, and see that you do not do the same. Above all things, little brother, prepare yourself, as I am doing, by prayer."

Karthar Singh would have given the boy much more useful advice, but at that moment there was a loud curse outside the door, followed by, "Hi, you blackguard, what are you up to now? I'll soon put an end to your little tricks!" The Mohammedan gaoler opened the door of the cell and stood glaring angrily at Arjun: "A fine young scamp you are! First you keep your people rushing all over the district after you, and then (as if that were not enough), when we get you safely caged up out of mischief, you begin operations by talking with your precious friend in the next room!" He shut the door of the cell with a bang and hurried away. In the course of ten minutes he returned again, and opening the door bade Arjun follow him. "There," he said with a sneer as he put the boy in a cell at the other end of the long corridor, "talk as much as you like now; no one will disturb you."

CROSSING A RIVER ON A SKIN BOAT.

XI.

ARJUN IN PRISON.

THE few days in gaol were a great blessing to Arjun. Weeks of persecution and anxiety, together with the exciting events connected with the attempt to escape, had entirely worn him out. Indeed so shaken and nervous had he become that the slightest sound made him start and a harsh word almost reduced him to tears. The quiet change therefore in the Simla gaol, with the knowledge that nothing could happen until the day set for the trial, were indeed a God-send. He slept and slept until he had slept all the weariness out of his body. And when he was not sleeping he was at prayer, or trying to picture to himself what the scene would be like in the court-room. Often in his own village he had heard of that great court-room, and of the great judge-sahib, who sat on the high seat behind the table and "looked and looked at you, till you forgot all the stories you had intended to tell him, and came out with the very truth itself ".

"Thank goodness," thought Arjun, with a sigh, "the truth is just what I wish him to get out of me. Father will swear that I am not yet fourteen, and will demand that I be sent home with him, and that Karthar Singh be sent to prison for running away with me—at least, that is what he said to the officer when we were first brought here. God grant that the sahib will see how old I really am, and understand that I was not following Karthar Singh, but Christ, when I left home."

At last the day arrived—one of those bright, cold winter days, when the pine forests stand out rich and green on the mountain sides, and the sweet clear air reminds one that the snow will soon be falling.

Arjun had his breakfast, and shortly before ten o'clock was taken off to the court-room.

What a busy place it was! On all sides of the great building crowds of people were waiting. Many of them were the rugged folk of his own mountains, standing in little groups about their lawyers, and looking distrustfully at the bustling crowd. To them, as to him, it was a strange, new sight, and many of them doubtless wished from the bottom of their simple hearts that they were safely back in their quiet little villages among the hills.

The boy was led up some narrow stone stairs, and into a broad corridor, lighted all along one side by great windows, and full of more silent, waiting people. Up this corridor he was led toward a closed door at the other end, which opened from time to time to let some frightened-looking party of people go in or out. Beside the door stood a tall Punjabi in red and gold, whose business it seemed was to call out the names of those whose case the judge-sahib wished next to try. He was a most imposing-looking person, and the strained attention with which the people listened to his words made Arjun think that he must be a very important man indeed.

He was gazing at the Punjabi with open-eyed admiration, when suddenly he heard a voice which made him start with fear. It was the voice of his father, but so stern and hard in tone that it seemed more like that of a stranger. "Where is this boy?" Nihal Singh was saying. "I must see him for a minute before we are called inside."

"Is not that he standing with the guard near

the door?" asked his companion—evidently one of the Indian lawyers of Simla.

Without even answering the speaker, the Rajput strode over to his shrinking son. His face was dark, but his voice was cold and steady as he spoke to the boy. "Arjun," he said, "you have always been a son who knew to obey his father; you must obey me now; do you understand?"

"Yes, sir," answered the boy faintly.

"That worthless scoundrel Karthar Singh has practised Christian magic on you, so that you have entirely forgotten your duty to your family, your caste and your village. You must tell the judge-sahib that you were enchanted and brought away against your will. Do you understand me?"

"Yes, sir," said Arjun, "I understand."

"The Englishman will ask you your age," continued his father. "Remember, *you are not yet fourteen*, and you must tell him so." The fierce face of the Rajput was close to that of his son.

But Arjun was a Rajput too. "Sir," he said, looking bravely into the stern eyes of his father, "I am between sixteen and seventeen—you have told me so yourself, and have so registered me

SKIN BOATS AND PADDLES.

in the school register; how then am I to say that I am not yet fourteen?"

"Unworthy and faithless one," ground out the man between his teeth, "do you dare question my word, and refuse to obey me? I swear by my daughter, Arjun, that I will kill you rather than have you disgrace us all. No son of mine shall ever live to mix with vile beef-eating foreigners! Once more I ask you—will you promise me to——"

"Nihal Singh, son of Naranjan Singh, of Zahu, and Arjun, son of Nihal Singh, of Zahu," shouted the Punjabi, and the Rajput was not able to finish his sentence.

The door opened to let them enter, and Arjun found himself in a room different from anything that he had ever seen before. The high walls and ceiling were panelled in rich dark wood. On the left two great windows set high in the wall lighted the place. At the farther end was a raised platform, and upon this a great desk-like structure, behind which sat a sahib busily writing.

Outside the door was shouting, and the anxious moving crowd, and garish light on bare whitewashed walls. Inside the door all was changed. The quiet, almost empty, room, with the sahib sitting at the great desk at the other end, scratching busily away with his pen, seemed, indeed, to be part of another world.

Presently he laid down his pen, and looked up. A clerk handed him a sheet of paper, and motioned to the party to approach. At the same time another door opened, and Karthar Singh was brought in by a guard and led up to the desk.

The judge read the paper through with a frowning brow, and then looked keenly at the tall young Indian standing before him.

"Karthar Singh, Christian, son of Har Charan Singh, charged with unlawfully abducting Arjun Singh, Rajput, son of Nihal Singh, aged 13 years 8 months, from his father's house," etc. etc. So the charge ran.

"Where is the plaintiff?" asked the judge.

"Here, your honour," said the Indian lawyer, leading Nihal Singh in front of the desk, "and he has retained me as counsel."

The lawyer was then told to make the charge, and proceeded to do so at once. He told how the Rajput had desired to give his son a good education, and how he had sent him to read at the Mission-school, at the same time ordering him to have as little as possible to do with the

Christians. "There," said he, "the poor child fell under the influence of the accused, who succeeded, by means of promises to show him the wonders of the plains, and by other cunning devices inducing him to run away from his home. His father followed the pair to Simla, and arrived just in time to prevent them from escaping by the train."

In conclusion the lawyer begged the judge to empower the father forcibly to take his son home, since the boy was not yet fourteen, and to sentence the accused for having unlawfully enticed away from the care of his lawful guardian one who in the eyes of the law was still a minor.

The case was well put, but the judge was a man trained by long experience in Indian law-courts, and he knew that all the parties in such a case would have to be heard if justice was to be done. He therefore told Nihal Singh to tell his own story.

"Your honour," said the Rajput, "the lawyer has told it all to you already. In an evil moment I sent my son—my only son—to the school of the Christians, hoping that he would there get a training which would fit him to be an honour and support to his home and to me in my old age. He was a good and obedient boy, but his stay at the school completely spoiled him. I do not know by what medicine or magic charms they took away his reason; all I know is that he forgot he was a Rajput, forgot that he was my son, and followed this fellow to Simla. He is not yet fourteen, and I beg you to allow me to take him home, and keep him safely locked up until he has come to his senses again."

"Where is the lad?" asked the judge abruptly. Arjun came forward, and stood beside Karthar Singh.

"Your name is Arjun Singh?" the Englishman asked.

"Yes, your honour," said Arjun, remembering to use the form of address adopted by his father and the lawyer.

"Now, Arjun Singh," said the judge in a kindly voice, "tell me why you ran away from home."

Our Lord Jesus told His followers not to be anxious about what they would say when taken before kings and rulers for His sake; "for," said He, "it will be given you in that hour what ye shall say".

And so it seemed with Arjun now. All his fear left him, and he felt as if the words he spoke

HUNTING TIGERS IN THE MOUNTAINS NEAR KOTGURH.

were given him by one stronger and wiser than himself.

"Sir," he said, "I ran away from home because my father would not let me serve Jesus Christ there. It is true that I came to love Him while at the Mission-school, and that I wished to become a Christian; but it is not true that I ran away from home on the persuasion of Karthar Singh." He then told the judge all the story of how he had been taken home and how pressure had been put upon him to make him forsake Christ, and how he had decided to run away, and had persuaded the young Sikh convert to help him.

"How old are you, boy?" asked the judge.

"Between sixteen and seventeen," he answered. "If you do not believe me, you will find that I am registered in this way in the entrance register of the school by my father."

The judge wrote something on a slip of paper, then calling one of the clerks he said, "Take this boy to Dr. H——. He is at present in the room at the other end of the corridor. Bring him back as soon as the Dr. Sahib has finished his examination."

While the boy was away Karthar Singh was given a hearing, and this judge found his heart going out to the simple, earnest young Indian who had suffered so much for his Master.

In about ten minutes the clerk returned with Arjun, and a note from the doctor.

The magistrate read it, and then taking up his pen commenced to write.

For nearly ten minutes the scratch of his pen was all that could be heard, then he turned to the people grouped in front of his desk and read the following: "I find that Arjun Singh is not a minor in the eyes of the law, having been pronounced by the doctor to be without doubt more than fourteen years old. The case of 'abduction' against Karthar Singh therefore falls to the ground.

"The boy Arjun Singh, being over fourteen, and having demonstrated to my satisfaction that he has an intelligent grasp of the doctrine of Christianity, I pronounce free to return to his village with his father, or proceed to the plains with his companion Karthar Singh, as was his first intention, etc. etc.

"(Signed) H. F.,

"*Magistrate.*"

XII.

A FINAL DECISION.

A MOMENT of absolute silence followed. The boy and his father, not fully comprehending the judicial decision, gazed anxiously at the magistrate. On the lad's face was an expression of timid yet earnest appeal; upon that of the father a look of fierce expectation. And indeed it was a critical moment in the life of each of them.

"My boy," said the judge in a kindly voice, leaning towards Arjun as he spoke, "you are free to choose for yourself. Think carefully, for you are taking a most serious step. Will you go home with the father who has loved you and cared for you all these years, or will you leave here with your friend, homeless and fatherless? Will you leave him who has sheltered you all your life to shift for himself in his old age, or will you return to Zahu, and be a true son to him? Think carefully, for your going will break your father's heart, and bring dishonour on his home."

It was in truth a solemn moment in the boy's life. Do not wonder, my reader, that even after having left home and suffered so much for Christ, he hesitated for a moment. His mind carried him away to the little village back among the hills, he saw the deserted home, and his father leading a lonely old age, deprived of the support and comfort of his son. He saw the gathering clouds of trouble, which would break on the rapidly whitening head of the old Rajput, as soon as people learned that he had lost his son. How would the ceaseless demands of the creditors be met, and the mouths of hereditary enemies be stopped? No wonder the heart of the poor boy ached, at the thought of taking a step which would plunge his aged parent into such trouble.

Nihal Singh was looking at his son with hungry eyes, too proud to plead, but unable to hide the longing of his heart. Nervously he fingered the back of the chair by which he stood, waiting breathlessly for the decision of the boy. At a little distance from him stood Karthar Singh, his head bowed in silent prayer. Arjun stood by himself, gazing with troubled face into the eyes of his father.

But God had not so lovingly carried His little lamb over many mountains and through many

ST. STEPHEN'S COLLEGE, DELHI.

dangers to forsake him in this hour of trial. Down in the heart of the boy a voice seemed speaking—that tender voice which had already called him so many weary miles from home. "Oh, Arjun," it seemed to say, "you can never be true to your father by being false to Me. I, too, love your father ; I poured out My blood for him on Calvary, and I have purposed to save him, through you, his son. Be brave, my little one. If you love him, then dare to break his heart. Take up your cross, and follow Me, as a true little soldier, assured that his salvation, as well as your own, depends upon it."

And like a true little Rajput, Arjun responded to the call of his Lord. Collecting himself with an effort he turned towards the magistrate. "Sir," he said, and his lip quivered, "I desire to become a Christian, and wish to accompany Karthar Singh."

It is needless to describe what followed. Nihal Singh made one more fierce, broken-hearted plea that his son might be given to him ; and, finding that nothing would change the judge's decision, left the court in sad silence. Karthar Singh led the boy, sobbing piteously, to the house of the old Christian who had received them upon their arrival in Simla, and on the following morning they left for the plains.

Six months later Arjun received baptism, in the same old Mission church in which Karthar had been made a member of the Body of Christ. Joyfully he pledged himself to "renounce the devil and all his works, the vain pomp and glory of the world, with all the covetous desires of the same, and the carnal desires of the flesh"; joyfully he promised, God being his helper, obediently to keep God's holy will and commandments, and walk in the same all the days of his life. Reverently and humbly he approached the font and received baptism. "In the name of the Father, and of the Son, and of the Holy Ghost".

"We receive this person into the congregation of Christ's flock," prayed the aged priest, "and do sign him with the sign of the Cross, in token that hereafter he shall not be ashamed to confess the faith of Christ crucified, and manfully to fight under His banner, against sin, the world, and the devil; and to continue Christ's faithful soldier and servant unto his life's end."

"Amen," murmured the boy earnestly, all the blood of his fighting ancestors thrilling an answer to the martial call contained in the ancient prayer, and there shone in his young eyes the light of a new and deeper spirit of consecration than had been there before—the purpose to "endure hardship as a good soldier of Jesus Christ," and to be of those of whom it is written that "they follow the Lamb whithersoever He goeth," loving not their life even unto death.

At last the service was ended, and Arjun left the church with Karthar Singh. There was no need of words, for each knew the thought of the other, and as they issued from the quiet churchyard into the midst of the noise and clatter of the busy world without, it seemed to them as if the din about them were a call to arms—a call to fight to the death against the powers of darkness which were crushing the soul out of the poor, hungry, heavy-laden world. And right bravely they responded to the call, and with high courage donned the armour of Christ, sallying forth on the road of pain and shame and dishonour in the footsteps of the Crucified.

XIII.

CONCLUSION.

AND now, my readers, you have heard all that I can tell you in this book of the story of Arjun, and I know that many of you will ask if it is a true story.

Although some of the facts in it are collected from the lives of other boys whom I know, the story is in the main a history of the life of a boy of the mountains. He learned to love Christ while reading in a Mission-school, he confessed in my presence and that of the schoolboys that he was about to follow Christ. He suffered weeks of persecution, and was carried off by his father to Zahu, the village I have so often spoken of here. At last he escaped one night with a friend, and after many hardships reached the plains where he received baptism. His life since then has been one of true advance in the love and service of Christ. He has at last won the heart of his father, and though he has not as yet

TWO OF THE STAFF AND THREE STUDENTS OF ST. STEPHEN'S COLLEGE, DELHI.

been able to draw the old Rajput to Christ, he nevertheless serves and cares for him as a dutiful son. If I were to let him know that I was writing such a story, I know that he would beg me to ask you to pray for the old man, that Christ should draw him away from Hindooism, and unite him with His flock.

Arjun has recently gone to S. Stephen's University College, Delhi, of which we give two illustrations.

And now in closing, I beg you to remember the people of the mountains in your prayers. Many are the hill-boys who desire to follow Christ, and many are the boys who would love Jesus if they only knew Him. Arjun is working for them; we are working for them; Karthar Singh is working for them. Will you not pray for them and for us? When you have grown older, and are able to choose the way in which you will serve God, some from among you may hear His voice in your hearts, calling you to come out and give your lives to the people of these mountains. Who can tell?